MOVING TO TAX-FREE

—————— MOVING TO ——————
TAX-FREE

Moving To Tax-Free LLC
www.movingtotaxfree.com
info@movingtotaxfree.com

ISBN: 979-8-9894209-0-2 (paperback)
ISBN: 979-8-9894209-1-9 (ebook)
ISBN: 979-8-9894209-2-6 (hardcover)
ISBN: 979-8-9894209-3-3 (audiobook)

Ordering Information:
Special discounts are available on quantity purchases by corporations, associations, and others. For details, contact info@movingtotaxfree.com or www.movingtotaxfree.com

Publisher's Cataloging-in-Publication Data

Names: Hosler, Bruce, 1960 - .
Title: Moving to tax-free : strategies for creating tax-free retirement income, and tax-free lifetime
        legacy income for your children / Bruce Hosler.
Description: Prescott, AZ : Moving to Tax-Free LLC, 2024. | Includes index.
Identifiers: ISBN 9798989420926 (hardback) | ISBN 9798989420902 (pbk) | ISBN 9798989420919
        (ebook) | ISBN 9798989420933 (audiobook)
Subjects: LCSH: Retirement – Planning. | Retirement income – United States. | Finance, Personal.
        | Tax planning. | BISAC: BUSINESS & ECONOMICS / Personal Finance / Taxation. | BUSINESS
        & ECONOMICS / Personal Finance / Money Management. | BUSINESS & ECONOMICS /
        Personal Finance / Retirement Planning.
Classification: LCC HG179.H67 2024 | DDC 332.024 H--dc23

MOVING TO TAX-FREE

STRATEGIES FOR CREATING TAX-FREE RETIREMENT INCOME,
AND TAX-FREE LIFETIME LEGACY INCOME FOR YOUR CHILDREN

BRUCE HOSLER

EA, CFP®, CPWA®, AIF®, CEPA®

WHAT OTHERS ARE SAYING ABOUT MOVING TO TAX-FREE

66 *Moving To Tax-Free* is worth a fortune to you in lifetime tax savings. In this one easy read, you will quickly profit from Bruce Hosler's years of knowledge and experience as he guides you along every possible path to a tax-free retirement!"

—ED SLOTT
CPA and retirement expert
Author and founder of www.irahelp.com
Founder of Ed Slott's Elite IRA Advisor Group[SM]

The statement was provided 3/1/24 by Ed Slott who is a nonclient and fellow financial professional. This statement may not be representative of the experience of others and is not a guarantee of future performance or success. For additional reviews, search us wherever local businesses are reviewed.

66 Where do you think tax rates are headed in the future? If you're like me, you know they are headed higher. After all, it's just math. Well, Eagle Scout Bruce Hosler is going to show you EXACTLY what to do to keep more of your hard-earned money. Learn simple techniques to reduce the #1 expense most seniors have—TAXES! *Moving to Tax-Free* is a book you will want to share with your entire family."

—TOM HEGNA
Author, speaker, economist, and TV host

The statement was provided 2/8/24 by Tom Hegna who is a nonclient and fellow financial professional. This statement may not be representative of the experience of others and is not a guarantee of future performance or success. For additional reviews, search us wherever local businesses are reviewed.

66 Bruce Hosler's thoughtful, well-written book raises a warning cry about the reality that tax rates, even ten years from now, are likely to be dramatically higher than they are today. He also spells out the dire consequences for a generation of Baby Boomers who have the lion's share of their retirement savings in tax-deferred investments like 401(k)s and IRAs. He then lays out a balanced, comprehensive strategy that not only shields you from tax-rate risk but protects you from an array of other retirement risks that can easily derail your retirement plan."

—DAVID MCKNIGHT
Author of *The Power of Zero*

The statement was provided 2/14/24 by David McKnight who is a nonclient and fellow financial professional. This statement may not be representative of the experience of others and is not a guarantee of future performance or success. For additional reviews, search us wherever local businesses are reviewed.

TABLE OF CONTENTS

CHAPTER 1

THE MOST IMPORTANT QUESTION

Will U.S. Tax Rates Be Higher in the Future?

"The hardest thing in the world to understand is the income tax."

—ALBERT EINSTEIN[1]

A wide variety of clients come into my office looking for guidance with their finances. They want to make sure their retirement savings will be enough to provide for the comfortable retirement they have always hoped for. They want to make sure their loved ones will be taken care of financially when they are gone.

One of the first questions we start with is the most important question. I ask them:

"When you look into the future over the next 10 years, do you think that tax rates in the United States will stay the same, go lower,

---

1   "Letters: Feb. 22, 1963," *Time*, February 22, 1963, https://content.time.com/time/subscriber/article/0,33009,827992-3,00.html.

or will they go higher?"

Almost all of them are surprised by my question. After a moment of consideration, almost in unison they chime in that they think the tax rates in the United States will go higher in the future.

I then ask them the second most important question. Why? Why do you believe the tax rates in the United States will be higher in the future? I receive a number of different answers:

- "It depends on which political party is in control."
- "It depends on who is in the White House."
- "Because of our national debt."
- "Because things always go up."
- "Because of inflation."
- As well as a few others.

Let me tell you right here and now, it does not matter which political party will be in control. For decades both political parties have voted to spend far more than the revenue we have coming in to the country's coffers.

I hope to show you in this book that there are five primary reasons that the federal government will have to raise taxes dramatically in the next 10 years.

Here are the reasons:

1. Interest on our ever increasing $34+ trillion national debt.

2. Inflation has caused the Fed to raise interest rates, so the interest rates that we must now pay on the national debt are much higher.

3. The Medicare Hospital Insurance Trust Fund is scheduled to run out of money in 2031.

4. The Social Security trust fund is scheduled to run out of money in 2033.

5. Our federal government continues to spend about $1.5 trillion dollars more each year than the revenues we have coming into the U.S. government, digging our national debt hole deeper and deeper each year.

Knowing the truth about these issues changes the importance of the question about future tax rates in the United States.

This is one of the most important questions I can ask anyone as we begin the process of setting up their financial plan, a plan that will not only provide them with a financially sound retirement but will also hopefully allow them to experience everything they have dreamed of throughout their working life.

My inquiry—will tax rates be higher in the future—is the essential question, and it is foundational to anyone's financial success in preparing for the retirement of their dreams. It's not surprising that most people I speak with believe that tax rates in the United States will be higher in the future than they are today, and this insight—the likelihood of higher future tax rates—is a very important piece of information to know and to consider. Possessing this knowledge allows you to change the entire direction of how you will approach saving for your retirement.

Consider the implications of the answer to the question. If future tax rates are higher than current tax rates, that means that ***current tax rates are on sale.***

Yes, you read that right: the current tax rates in the United States are on sale compared to future higher tax rates.

Now pause for a minute and consider how important having this piece of information is: you can plan to pay taxes now, at lower rates, while you have a chance to do so, with full knowledge of all the opportunities and options that such knowledge provides.

Once you realize the significance of the knowledge, that future tax rates in the United States will likely be much higher than today's rates, it makes sense to find ways to protect yourself and your family from those future higher tax rates.

The purpose and heart of this book is to help you strategically plan how you and your family can pay less taxes over your lifetime.

I want to help you create an intentional tax-reduction plan using advanced tax strategies that will help you to begin ***moving to tax-free.***

I hope to show you options available to not only save taxes when you retire but also potentially to live income tax–free from federal and state income taxes, improving the chance that you will have the retirement you have hoped for.

I know that you might feel skeptical, and that's understandable. But the information I am about to share with you works—you simply need to learn the ins and outs of our tax system, the legal tax breaks that are available to you, and how to systematically begin moving to tax-free.

I have helped my clients systematically move their financial affairs to tax-free vehicles. Some of them have stopped their Social Security from being taxed. When you can do that, it is a beautiful thing.

This information can help almost everyone, including financially successful and astute pre-retirees and retirees, business owners, executives, doctors, lawyers, and other professionals. These financially astute, educated, and sophisticated investors are looking for ways to minimize both their current and future income taxes.

Many of my clients are family stewards worried about their loved ones. They are trying to make sure they have planned for a transfer of their wealth to their children in the most tax-efficient manner possible. That is what this book is all about.

What Is "Tax-Free"?

In the tax code, there's no such thing as "tax-free." The IRS considers income vehicles that are exempt from federal income taxes to be simply "tax-exempt." But in my definition of "tax-free," what we're looking for is income that we can distribute from our investments in retirement that will be:

- income tax–free from Federal taxes,
- income tax–free from state taxes, and
- income tax–free from capital gains taxes.

Included in the definition of "tax-free" is the requirement that the income must not be included in the calculation to determine your provisional income. The provisional income calculation is used to determine the taxability of your Social Security benefits. That is, if you have too much provisional income, it can make your Social Security benefits taxable. But if you can arrange for all or most of your income sources to be income tax–free, your Social Security benefits could be income tax–free as well. That will be one of our primary goals for you: tax-free Social Security benefits.

We will cover many potential sources of tax-free income within this book, such as the Roth IRA and the Roth 401(k), the life insurance retirement plan (LIRP), the health savings account (HSA), the 529 plan to Roth IRA rollover, and the reverse mortgage line of credit.

Looking for Valhalla

"Let's go to Valhalla with the sun on our faces."

—MARK LAWRENCE[2]

In Norse mythology, Valhalla is the hall of slain warriors. They live there blissfully under the leadership of the god Odin. By definition, Valhalla represents the ultimate glory and happiness. Valhalla is the warriors' heaven, if you will.[3]

Why am I using a mythical place/concept when describing moving to tax-free? Some people initially don't believe tax-free income is even possible; to them it is nothing more than a mythical Valhalla.

I can assure you that tax-free income is very real. I have helped many clients achieve levels of tax-free income that they thought were unattainable.

---

2   Mark Lawrence, *Prince of Fools: The Red Queen's War: Book One* (New York: Ace Books, 2014), 360.

3   Noah Tetzner, "Valhalla: How Viking Belief in a Glorious Afterlife Empowered Warriors," History, March 3, 2021, https://www.history.com/news/viking-valhalla-valkyrie-afterlife.

Moving to tax-free is a simple concept. We break down your assets, income, IRAs, and other retirement accounts and start strategically moving them into the tax-free investment vehicles. We are seeking the ever-elusive Valhalla. In your financial case, Valhalla is a combination of tax-free vehicles that we can use in concert to generate all the tax-free income you will need in retirement.

The Roth IRA is one such vehicle. Roth IRA distributions are not included in your taxable income, provided you are 59 and one-half and have funded a Roth IRA at least five years ago. Additionally, they don't trigger taxability of your Social Security benefits. This can help keep your other taxable income sources in a lower tax bracket because your Roth IRA income is tax-free. It does not add to your adjusted gross income (AGI). In turn, such income does not subject your Medicare benefits to premium penalties like IRMAA (income-related monthly adjustment amount) because your income is too high. Think of IRMAA as just one example of how the government has already started to raise the tax rates on high-income earners receiving Medicare benefits by adding an extra tax.

Valhalla may be a myth, but I like the comparison because finding Valhalla seems impossible, just like tax-free income seems impossible. But it is possible to move portions of your income to tax-free income. I have been able to make this a reality for my clients, and I can make tax-free income a reality for you too, helping you work toward the retirement of your dreams.

Throughout this book, I will use hypothetical case studies to illustrate my point. These case studies do not represent actual clients. The case studies should not be construed as a recommendation. Your experience may vary, and you should always consult qualified tax and financial professionals for your individual situation. This is an example of what I do for my clients.

Let me share a hypothetical example of how I would implement tax-planning strategies with a client.

John had $2 million in his traditional IRA account; he'd been saving for years and had always thought his retirement was going to be wonderful, especially when it came to having enough money. But doubt crept in.

He became concerned about what was going on with the United States government—with the national debt, the way the country was spending money, etc. He was concerned that there could be a great disruption, not just with the country, but with his portfolio. He became concerned about the likelihood that his tax rates would go higher, maybe even *much* higher.

With $2 million in his traditional IRA, his thinking was, "Wow, I'm going to convert this whole thing [IRA to a Roth IRA] all at once, pay the taxes, and be done with it." He figured that was the best way to keep his future secure.

When he came to talk to me about tax planning, I told him, "Wait a minute. Is this the end of the world as you see it? Do you think the tax rates are going to explode to an all-time high soon? Is this going to happen this year or next year? In the next three or four years?"

He was a little less sure about the timing, but he felt like he wanted to get it over with and be done with it.

I told him, "The tax rates from the Tax Cuts and Jobs Act of 2017 are very generous right now. You can begin converting $200,000 or $300,000 a year from your IRA to a Roth IRA. And if you strategically convert that amount to your Roth IRA every year and do this over a number of years instead of all at once, you could potentially save (13% in federal and 3% state taxes—federal currently 37% tax bracket versus 24% tax bracket) federal and state income tax rates by being strategic and using the tax bracket strategy over a period of time."

••

It's a myth that if you're going to convert your IRA to a Roth, you have to do it all at once. Unfortunately, a lot of people believe that myth. That was John's initial belief. He didn't know that he could make a partial IRA to Roth conversion each year and strategically move those funds to a tax-free Roth IRA systematically over a number of years. When converting money from an IRA to a Roth IRA, you recognize taxable income on the amount you convert in the year of the conversion; however, by breaking it up over the span of several years, you can strategically arrange your income to stay in lower tax brackets, allowing you to convert your IRA to a Roth IRA in a lower tax bracket. That will save you tax dollars in making the conversion.

John agreed to convert his money over the span of several years, keeping his effective tax bracket at 24%, which in 2024 includes taxable income of $201,051 to $383,900 for those filing married filing jointly (MFJ). He would have been paying taxes in the 37% tax bracket, which in 2024 starts at $731,201 taxable income for MFJ, plus more in state taxes depending on his state if he had converted the whole IRA account all at once like he was planning. Finding financial Valhalla might not be as easy for you as it was for John, but **moving to tax-free** (or as close to it as possible) is a very real thing.

Let's get started.

CHAPTER 2

WHAT DRIVES ME TO WANT TO HELP YOU

A Little Background About Me

🔑

"Our distrust is very expensive."

—RALPH WALDO EMERSON

In 1972, the year that I turned 12 years old, my dad started his Native American arts and crafts store in the southwestern United States. That year, Sonny and Cher were on TV wearing big squash blossom necklaces and concho belts. Native American art and jewelry were very popular.

My dad had a banner year and ended up with about $10,000 of extra profit (that would equate to about $50,000-plus today after adjusting for inflation). He didn't know where to invest the money.

I grew up in a very small town. It didn't even have a real stoplight, just a flashing red light. The population was only about 3,500 people. I was the oldest of six kids. My dad didn't have a financial advisor. I'm not even sure how he would have gone about finding a competent financial advisor or tax professional back then.

One day, a man came to town promoting sugar options as the best investment to make at that time. He told my dad it was a no-lose proposition. My dad was going to make a killing for sure.

This was a *sure thing*, the man told my father. A safe bet. A chance to make some real money.

My dad invested the entire $10,000 into sugar options.

If you buy bonds, the principal you invest is generally pretty safe, and you can collect a little interest. With stocks, they can go up and down, but even if they lose some value, they will probably still hold the majority of their value.

But if you buy an option…it has a time value, and then it decays, and it can expire, worthless.

And that's exactly what happened.

My dad lost all the money he invested in the sugar option. Needless to say, Christmas that year was not the same. Things were difficult for our family. My father never forgot that experience.

The most damaging thing was the realization that my family didn't have anybody we could trust with our finances. There was no advisor looking out for our family, guiding us to make the right decisions.

This experience damaged my father from that point forward in his life. He never trusted anyone with his money ever again. His go-to investment since then has been raw land. Why? Because no one can pick it up and steal it from him. Unfortunately for my dad, raw land can be one of the worst investments you can imagine.

Unlike developed land, where you can normally put 20% down and get financing for the rest, raw land generally requires you to pay all cash up front. Additionally, if you buy normal rental income property—developed land with a building on it—you can receive rental income as well as tax-advantaged income because you get to depreciate the building.

On raw land, my dad does not receive rental income, cannot get tax deductions for depreciation on the land, and has to pay all cash up front because you can't really get a loan for raw land. He does not receive any of the good benefits that an investment in real estate will normally provide.

He has purchased a number of little pieces of raw land that have hardly appreciated over the years.

He has been hesitant to invest in other ways because he simply doesn't trust anyone. Even though I am a CFP® professional, he just can't bring himself to trust a mutual fund, or an exchange-traded fund, or even individual stocks. He was burned so badly he does not trust any of the American companies that form the U.S. equity markets, bond markets, or any commercial investment vehicle. Fortunately, he did participate in his 401(k) at work, and that worked very well for him.

I've seen firsthand how the lack of trusted financial advice and financial planning can affect a family, and it's one of the reasons that I entered this business—I want to make sure that no family goes through what my family went through, receiving poor advice from a charlatan.

I'm trying to help protect people from the biggest cost we will have: taxes.

That's been one of my biggest motivations in this business, and it's why I gravitated toward this career.

Even with my experience as a family accountant and the family financial advisor, my dad still can't overcome his skepticism of the financial markets. His ability to trust them has been broken. He can't bring himself to trust other people or any financial organization. I have met other people as well who have been hurt so badly that they cannot overcome their mistrust and doubt. They have become doubtful just like my father, and it's so sad, because with just a little bit of trust, they could be helped.

I have been practicing now for more than 27 years as a tax accountant (an Enrolled Agent (EA)—that is, an accountant who specializes in taxes) and a CERTIFIED FINANCIAL PLANNER™ professional. In these capacities I have worked with hundreds of families. Bringing tax planning, financial planning, estate planning, insurance planning, and retirement income planning together has allowed me to see and implement some of the best integrated financial strategies available for my clients.

Because of my multiprofessional credentials, training, expertise, and experience, I'm in a good position to provide you with high-level tax and financial-planning advice. In the coming chapters, I've detailed everything I think you should know about the move to tax-free so you can be prepared for the challenges that will certainly appear in the coming years. I am hoping to help you make decisions that will help you and your family lower your tax burden and experience the future you've always dreamed of.

CHAPTER 3

BE PREPARED

The Principles of Personal Finance and Tax Planning

"The ability to discipline yourself to delay gratification in the short term in order to enjoy greater rewards in the long term, is the indispensable prerequisite for success."

—BRIAN TRACY

"Self-respect is the root of discipline: The sense of dignity grows with the ability to say no to oneself."

—ABRAHAM JOSHUA HESCHEL[4]

A Guardian Angel—Named "Angel"

The work I perform for my clients sometimes makes me feel a little bit like a guardian angel.

---

4   Abraham Joshua Heschel, *The Insecurity of Freedom* (New York: Farrar, Straus and Giroux, 1966), 44.

It reminds me of something that happened when I was a Varsity Coach, a leader of Boy Scouts ages 14 and 15 years old. Our troop drove all the way from Prescott, Arizona, to Beaver, Utah, for a camp, where we stayed for eight days. We drove up in two trucks, and the drive took us through Las Vegas, through the desert, and all the way up into the mountains at an elevation of 9,000 feet. It was beautiful, lush, and green.

After eight days of camping, we started heading back. I was driving an old truck across the Nevada desert, and it was about 115 degrees out there when the truck overheated. We had to pull off the freeway before we got to Las Vegas.

The thermostat had frozen closed, so the coolant was not circulating properly, and the engine was overheating.

Steam was coming out from under the hood, so we took our cooler of water and poured some of it on the radiator to cool things off.

We didn't really know what to do.

And then, out of nowhere, in the middle the Nevada desert, a man named Angel showed up and offered to help us. He might as well have been a guardian angel—he happened to be a mechanic. Where we had some tools and some know-how, he had the proper tools and knew exactly what we needed to do.

He proceeded to disconnect the hose that connected the engine to the radiator, and he pulled out the thermostat that was stuck closed and put it all back together without the thermostat. He provided us with just enough water to top off our radiator. Angel was the answer to our prayers.

As a financial advisor, I sometimes feel like an angel—helping people plan financially, invest prudently, and minimize taxes in ways that are far beyond their own ability. In some cases, our work saves people from their own worst impulses. It's an amazing feeling to be responsible for guiding people to a successful retirement. It makes all my professional work worthwhile.

The strategies I share can be life changing for the people we serve. In a financial way, we become guardian angels for our clients and their loved ones.

The Boy Scout Personal Management Merit Badge

I have spent many years involved with the Boy Scouts. I earned my Eagle Scout award as a boy, and my two brothers did as well. Both of my sons are also Eagle Scouts. I love and have lived the principles of the Scout Law my entire life. The 12 principles of the Boy Scout Law are *trustworthy, loyal, helpful, friendly, courteous, kind, obedient, cheerful, thrifty, brave, clean,* and *reverent.*[5]

Another bedrock principle of the Boy Scouts is the Boy Scout motto, "Be Prepared,"[6] which also happens to be a core focus of retirement planning.

As an adult, I served as a Boy Scout leader in some capacity for almost 36 years, and until recently, I served as a personal manage-

---

5   "What Are the Scout Oath and Scout Law?," Boy Scouts of America, accessed April 30, 2023, https://www.scouting.org/about/faq/question10/.

6   Bryan Wendell, "Be Prepared: The Origin Story Behind the Scout Motto," Aaron on Scouting, May 8, 2017, https://blog.scoutingmagazine.org/2017/05/08/be-prepared-scout-motto-origin.

ment merit badge counselor. In that role, I taught young men the importance of financial principles. I would like to discuss a couple of those concepts with you now.

What Is Saving?

When I ask people the question, "What is saving?" I get a lot of different answers. Some answers deal with bank savings accounts or different investments that they may put money into. I want you to really think about the question. *What is saving?*

Saving is the act of living on less than you earn and setting the difference aside and not spending it. Saving is the act of living beneath your means purposefully. It is the seed for the creation of wealth.

Let me say that again. **Saving is the seed for the creation of wealth.**

If you get your paycheck and spend it all, you have saved nothing. If you get your paycheck and put 10% of it into your savings account, that is the act of saving.

Unless you learn the principle of saving and build the ability to set something aside for a future day and time, you will never be able to achieve your financial goals.

Learning to save is a financial success principle and skill that differentiates financial success from financial failure.

People save their money in different ways and store their savings in different places. When you were a child, you may have saved your money in a piggy bank or tin can. People save their money in safes and under their mattresses. And of course, many people save their money in bank accounts. Checking accounts are typically used for day-to-day purposes, while savings accounts are more suited for setting money aside.

What Is Investing?

You have to save money before you can invest it.

Investing is the process of deciding where you will place your savings, with the intention of seeing your money grow.

You can invest your savings in a savings account at the bank or in a certificate of deposit. You can invest your savings into any number of financial instruments, including stocks, bonds, exchange-traded funds (ETFs), mutual funds, real estate, commodities, or cryptocurrencies.

Although asset allocation programs cannot guarantee an objective, studies have shown that investment asset allocation can affect as much as 93% of the success of your investments.[7] Some people seek instant gratification with their investments, while others are more deliberate and can plan for delayed gratification. Let's talk more about these principles.

We Live in a World of Instant Gratification

We live in a world of fast food, social media, Netflix binge-watching,

---

7   Gary P. Brinson, L. Randolph Hood, and Gilbert L. Beebower, "Determinants of Portfolio Performance," *Financial Analysts Journal* 42, no. 4 (1986): 39–44, https://www.jstor.org/stable/4478947.

banking from our phones, Google searches, Amazon shopping, and e-filing our taxes.

Everything in life is focused on now, now, now. We have become addicted to impatience and do not tolerate anything that causes a delay or inconvenience.

I use and enjoy all the creature comforts just like the next person. Certainly, they have made us more efficient and more productive. But I fear that people are becoming desensitized to the reality that some things require time, patience, diligence, and perseverance.

Strategic tax-planning and tax-reduction strategies cannot be accomplished instantaneously. They require time, patience, diligence, perseverance, and strategic intent, with a dedicated process that, over time, will help the taxpayer achieve their goals.

You Must Practice the Art of "Delayed Gratification"

If you wanted to create a brand-new apple orchard or grape vineyard, you wouldn't expect to plant the seeds one month and then harvest your crop the next. Such thinking runs contrary to nature and reality. The farmer plants, waters, nurtures, fertilizes, and prunes, and he will then have to wait years before his crop is ready to harvest.

When financially planning for your retirement, patience and diligence will win the day.

That is what I am inviting you to do: to provide for your own tax-free future, using practice, patience, and diligence.

The move to tax-free cannot be achieved in an instant—there's no easy way to catch up. And even if you are uber-successful, even if you're an overnight TikTok sensation, you cannot move to tax-free in one year.

No, this is a longer-term process to strategically begin moving in the direction of tax-free.

That's why I named the book *Moving to Tax-Free* and not *Moved to Tax-Free*—you can't just do this all at once. For real success, you have to strategically implement this type of planning over a number of years.

If you convert your whole traditional IRA to a Roth in one year, you're going to pay the highest maximum tax, 37%, on all that money, or most of it, when you make such a conversion. If you take four or five years to convert your IRA to a Roth IRA, then you might be able to lower your tax rate to the 24% tax bracket and save yourself 13% in federal taxes, which can then be left to grow tax-free for years and decades to come. That can add up to a lot of money. And that's far more favorable for your future retirement.

The Sooner You Start, the Better

If you're just starting the move to tax-free at age 65, that does not give you very long. The sooner you begin, the better your potential outcome.

Imagine I have a pair of hypothetical clients who are in their 70s. I view them as my poster children for moving to tax-free. They've been at it for five or six years, and we're getting close to having them moved all the way to tax-free. The couple worked overseas in China for years, and they made $250,000 a year. And now we are going to be able to get them to the point where they will be able to take approximately $200,000 annually of combined tax-free income out of their life insurance plans and out of their Roth IRAs. If we are successful, their $60,000 of joint Social Security benefits will become income tax–free as well.

They will potentially generate around $250,000 a year in annual income and will not have to pay income tax on any of it.

Unfortunately, people who own pensions or own rental real estate most likely won't be able to get to a point where 100% of their income will qualify to be income tax–free the way that this couple will. But it's very powerful to be able to move as far as possible toward tax-free income. It can change your life when you retire if you do not have to pay income tax on your Social Security benefits.

Failure to Plan

What's your tax plan for the rest of your life? Do you have one?

If you do not have a tax plan, you will receive the default plan, the government plan. It's the one the government chooses for you. Do you feel they have your best interest in mind?

If you fail to plan for tax-free income, your lack of tax planning will give you the government plan, and that, my friends, is not the plan you will want.

CHAPTER 4

"HOUSTON, WE HAVE A PROBLEM."

Tax Rates in the United States Are on Sale—Right Now

*"Their moon-bound spacecraft wrecked by an oxygen tank explosion on April 13, 1970, the astronauts urgently radioed, **'Houston, we've had a problem here.'***

*Screenwriters for the 1995 film Apollo 13 wanted to punch that up. Thus was born, **'Houston, we have a problem.'"***

—MARCIA DUNN[8]

America, we have a problem!

As a country, we're not paying down the national debt or even keeping it level. At the end of 2023, the national debt was higher than it's ever been, above $34 trillion—that's 34 followed by 12

---

8   Marcia Dunn, "Apollo 13's Most Famous Quotes Originated in Hollywood," AP News, April 9, 2020, https://apnews.com/article/il-state-wire-technology-us-news-tx-state-wire-europe-c17fd5526198f00139b097452206bc77.

zeros.[9] We are adding one to two trillion dollars or more to that massive figure every year.

In December of 2023 the national debt exceeded $34 trillion. The government continues to overspend what income it has coming in, pushing off the growing problem in an endless loop of financial mismanagement.

In order to provide you with some context as to how out of control our national debt is, please consider the government's own chart on our national debt over the last 100 years. Please note how dramatically it has grown in the last 20 years. (See chart on the next page.)

David M. Walker, the former comptroller general of the United States—the top accountant for the country—has stated, "The federal government has lost control of our national finances." He considers the current budget system "badly broken."[10] This is a view shared by many financial experts, leading economists, and university economics professors.

In his book *Comeback America: Turning the Country Around and Restoring Fiscal Responsibility*, Walker warns us of what the coming tax rates will have to be in America.

Let's assume that Washington policy makers continue to punt on making tough spending choices and ultimately raise taxes to address the growing deficits. Nobody will reach in our kids'

---

9   Hanna Ziady and Tami Luhby, "US National Debt Hits Record $34 Trillion," CNN Business, last updated January 3, 2024, https://www.cnn.com/2024/01/03/economy/us-national-debt-34-trillion/index.html.

10 David M. Walker, "It Is Time to Confront Fiscal Failure," *The Hill*, June 27, 2019, https://thehill.com/opinion/finance/450674-it-is-time-to-confront-fiscal-failure/.

U.S. NATIONAL DEBT OVER THE LAST 100 YEARS

INFLATION ADJUSTED — 2022 DOLLARS

2022
FISCAL YEAR

$30.93 T
TOTAL DEBT

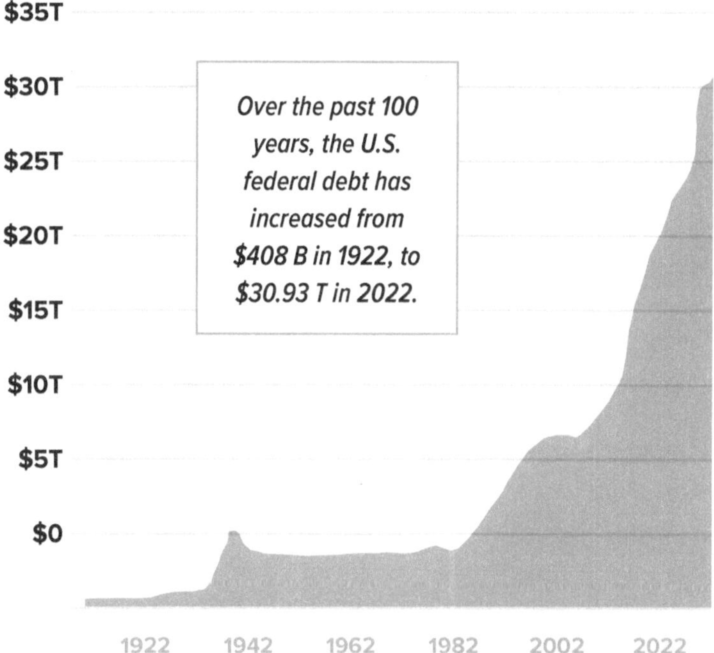

Visit the Historical Debt Outstanding dataset to explore and download this data. The inflation data is sourced from the Bureau of Labor Statistics.

Last Updated: *September 30, 2022*

*pockets and take their money because the government will take
it before it even reaches their pockets. What will that mean for
their after-tax income? Right now, on average, Americans pay
about 21 percent of their income in federal taxes, and another
10 percent to state and local governments. By 2030, to pay our
rising bills, that amount could be at least 45 percent—higher
even than the average 42 percent that most Europeans pay. By
2040, it would be at least 53 percent and climbing.*

*In reality, total taxes in 2030 and 2040 would be even higher
than these estimates because of the fiscal challenges facing state
and local governments—such as Medicaid costs, unfunded
retiree health care promises, underfunded pension plans,
deferred maintenance and other critical infrastructure needs,
and higher education funding.*[11]

Did you read that right? At least 45% by 2030 and 53% by 2040.

Wow! The American people I know are not prepared for the coming tax hikes.

You might be wondering how Walker can project these numbers
with such accuracy about future tax rates. It's because it is just math,
and math is very accurate.

The interest required to service our national debt is growing. And
now the high inflation we have had in 2022 and 2023 and the higher
interest rates that the Federal Reserve implemented will compound
the problem of paying the interest due each year on our national

---

11 David M. Walker, *Comeback America: Turning the Country Around and Restoring Fiscal
Responsibility* (New York: Random House, 2010), 19.

debt. Every other area of the federal budget is going to get squeezed because so much revenue will be required to pay the interest due on our federal debt.

Imagine your tax rates doubling to 50% of every dollar you earn. Yes, 50%. That is likely a tax rate the government will require of you to maintain their spending requirements.

The government won't be able to push this problem off much longer. The country has been living well beyond its means for far too long, and in the coming years, we will have to pay for all our excessive government spending in the United States.

You may think, "Bruce, this is hogwash." But consider what other experts are saying.

The bipartisan Committee for a Responsible Federal Budget (CRFB), led by President Maya MacGuineas, released a report titled the *Risks and Threats from Deficits and Debt* in 2022, noting how "the U.S. national debt is higher as a share of Gross Domestic Product (GDP) than at any time since World War II and is on course to breach that record."[12]

A separate article from CRFB explored whether the U.S. could fix its debt by taxing the top 1%—but in fact, raising the two top tax brackets to rates of 100% wouldn't even raise enough revenue to fully resolve the issue.[13]

---

12 "Risks and Threats from Deficits and Debts," Committee for a Responsible Federal Budget, July 14, 2022, https://www.crfb.org/papers/risks-and-threats-deficits-and-debt.

13 "What Would the Top Income Tax Rate Need to Be to Achieve Certain Fiscal Targets in 2025?," Committee for a Responsible Federal Budget, accessed April 30, 2023, https://www.crfb.org/sites/default/files/taxes%20on%201%20percent%20ffc.PNG.

WHAT WOULD THE TOP INCOME TAX RATE NEED TO BE TO ACHIEVE CERTAIN FISCAL TARGETS IN 2025?

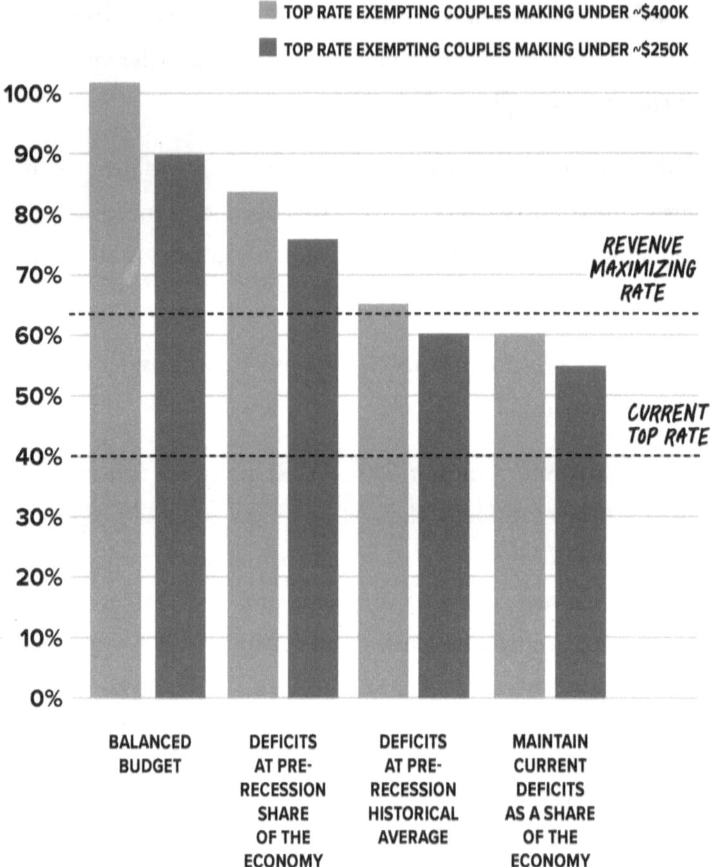

Source: CBO, JCT, CRFB Calculations

Note: Roughly Calculated Revenue Maximizing Income Tax Rate of 63%

Based on Diamond-Saez revenue maximizing rate adjusted for state/local and non-income taxes

So how high will tax rates have to increase to allow us to pay for the debt and all the other expenses necessary to run our government? The math is scary. See the chart on the previous page.

Folks, did you see the footnote?

The top tax rate would have to be 63% by 2025 in order to achieve certain fiscal targets. You may be thinking, "Oh, the tax rates will never go that high." Are you serious?

What do you think the historical tax rates look like in the United States? Look at the chart on the next page.

I am telling you, tax rates in the United States are on sale—right now.

Tax rates will have to increase dramatically to pay the national debt and the growing amount of interest on that debt, and they will have to increase *substantially* in order to just sustain our underfunded social insurance programs like Social Security and Medicare.[14]

How much of that tax increase you will have to pay during your retirement depends on how you plan *right now*. A tax tsunami is going to crash upon American taxpayers sometime between now and 2034 (when both the Medicare and the Social Security trust funds have been depleted). Please, please, let this be your warning, your siren, your call to action to make changes to your personal finances in order to prepare for what lies ahead.

Financial experts have been warning about the incoming tax

---

14 "Can We Fix the Debt Solely by Taxing the Top 1 Percent?," Committee for a Responsible Federal Budget, August 6, 2015, https://www.crfb.org/blogs/can-we-fix-debt-solely-taxing-top-1-percent.

HIGHEST FEDERAL MARGINAL INDIVIDUAL INCOME TAX RATE

TAX YEAR 1913-2020

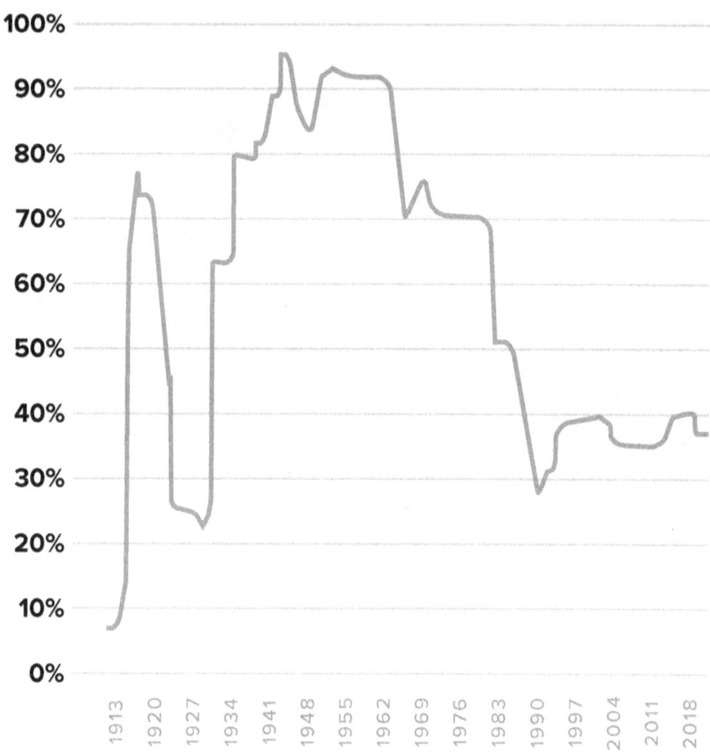

Sources: *Joseph Pechman, Federal Tax Policy; Joint Committee on Taxation, Summary of Conference Agreement on the Jobs and Growth Tax Relief Reconciliation Act of 2003, JCX-54-03, May 2003; IRS Revenue Procedures, various years.*

Notes: *This figure contains a number of simplificiations and ignores factors such as the amount of income or types of income subhead too the top rates, or the value of standard and itemized deductions.*

wave for years.

The organization Truth in Accounting publishes trackers on its website that quantify the "published" national debt (again, $34 trillion plus in late 2023) as well as "the truth," which factors in Social Security benefits and Medicare and other promises and obligations for American citizens.[15] They show the truth about our debt to be more like $159 trillion as of September 2023.

The national debt doesn't tell the full story or represent the full liabilities of the U.S. government.

It's impossible for our country to pay all the costs we are facing as a nation, and it's likely going to require a combination of cutting social insurance benefits and raising taxes—not just for the wealthy, but for every American in every income bracket. And even after all of that, we will still need to take additional drastic measures to cut costs and increase revenue.

Looking Ahead

As if that wasn't foreboding enough, ITR Economics, one of the leading economic forecasters operating today, predicted that the next Great Depression is going to begin in 2030 and last for about 10 years. Among the causes cited are demographics, health care costs, entitlements, inflation, aging population, and the increasing U.S. national debt.[16]

---

15 "Our Debt Clock," Truth in Accounting, accessed April 30, 2023, https://www. truthinaccounting.org/about/our_national_debt.

16 "Top 5 Causes of the 2030s Great Depression," ITR Economics, May 20, 2022, https:// blog.itreconomics.com/blog/top-5-causes-2030s-great-depression.

The possibility of a depression is a difficult but important consideration.

And it makes the move to tax-free all the more important—because the more you can do now to move to tax-free, the better off you'll be in the future when the tough times (like a worldwide depression) arrive.

Here is what Brian Beaulieu and Alan Beaulieu, the founders of ITR Economics and the authors of the book *Prosperity in the Age of Decline*, have to say about who the "(Potential) Losers" will be in the times ahead.

> *Taxpayers. Reduce benefits or raise taxes will be the primary choices confronting politicians. The path of least resistance will be to increase taxes on the rich. That is an interesting concept because politicians will get to decide who the rich are. Most likely they will construe the rich as those with higher incomes or with substantial assets. The rich today pay most of the taxes the government receives. Get ready to pony up even more money in the future.*[17]

Some of you may be thinking, "Well, we need more revenue; we are not raising enough revenue." Our country is raising more revenue now than it ever has before—even with our currently historically low tax rates.

Consider the government's own reporting of our national revenues:

---

17 Brian Beaulieu and Alan Beaulieu, *Prosperity in The Age of Decline: How to Lead Your Business and Preserve Wealth Through the Coming Business Cycles* (Hoboken, NJ: Wiley, 2014), 67.

FEDERAL REVENUE TRENDS OVER TIME, FY 2015-2022

INFLATION ADJUSTED — 2022 DOLLARS

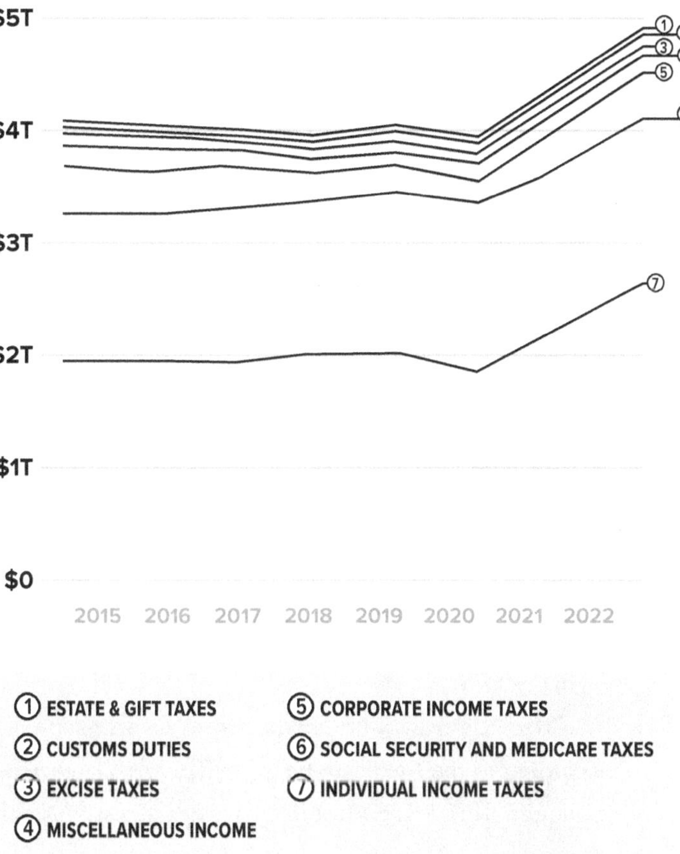

1. ESTATE & GIFT TAXES
2. CUSTOMS DUTIES
3. EXCISE TAXES
4. MISCELLANEOUS INCOME
5. CORPORATE INCOME TAXES
6. SOCIAL SECURITY AND MEDICARE TAXES
7. INDIVIDUAL INCOME TAXES

Note: Total revenue has increased from $4.05T in 2015 to $4.90T in 2022.

Visit the Monthly Treasury Statement (MTS) dataset to explore and download this data. The inflation data is sourced from the Bureau of Labor Statistics.

Last updated: September 30, 2022.

"In 2022, the U.S. government collected the highest total revenue in its history."[18]

What does all this mean??

Some of Our Country's Many Financial Challenges

Please consider just a few of the financial challenges we are facing as a country. These challenges will likely cause our government to take steps to raise taxes to meet these financial challenges.

- With interest rates having been held low deliberately, the annual cost of interest in the national debt has been sustainable up to this point. When the Federal Reserve raises interest rates rapidly due to the devaluation of our currency, the burden of servicing the higher interest payments on all of our national debt will force politicians to seek more tax revenue to cover the higher costs. As interest rates remain higher than they have been in the recent past, the pain we will experience to service the national debt will appear in the form of higher—much higher—taxes.

- The Medicare trust fund is expected to be depleted by 2028, according to the Medicare Board of Trustees's latest report to Congress. This would most likely narrow access to health care

---

18 "How Much Revenue Has the U.S. Government Collected This Year?," Fiscal Data: Treasury.Gov, accessed April 30, 2023, https://fiscaldata.treasury.gov/americas-finance-guide/government-revenue/.

benefits for millions of retired and disabled Americans.[19]

- The Social Security trust fund is projected to run out of money in approximately 2033.[20]

- The Tax Cuts and Jobs Act of 2017 will sunset in December of 2025. That means that without any action by Congress and the president, we will step up to the higher tax rates we had prior to the Tax Cuts and Jobs Act in 2017—an automatic tax increase without a single vote being cast.[21]

Why the Crisis Has Intensified

Consider President Joe Biden's budget for FY 2022,[22] which totals more than $6 trillion. Of that total:

- Social Security makes up nearly $1.2 trillion (nearly 20%).

- About $1.3 trillion (about 22%) is earmarked for either Medicare or Medicaid.

- Discretionary spending is almost $1.7 trillion, including $715 billion for defense spending.

- Interest on the national debt annually was $724 billion in 2022.

---

19 Robert King, "Medicare Hospital Trust Fund to Run Out of Money in 2028, Trustees Say," Fierce Healthcare, June 3, 2022, https://www.fiercehealthcare.com/providers/trustee-report-hospital-insurance-fund-run-out-money-2028.

20 Scott Horsley, "Social Security Is Now Expected to Run Short of Cash by 2033," NPR, March 31, 2023, https://www.npr.org/2023/03/31/1167378958/social-security-medicare-entitlement-programs-budget.

21 "Planning for the Tax Cuts and Jobs Act Sunset in 2025," Manning & Napier, January 6, 2023, https://www.manning-napier.com/insights/planning-for-the-tax-cuts-and-jobs-act-sunset-in-2025.

22 "Budget of the U.S. Government," The White House, https://www.whitehouse.gov/wp-content/uploads/2021/05/budget_fy22.pdf.

- And then there's another trillion or so that we have to borrow. That means print.

Tons of money is being poured into the Social Security and Medicare trust funds, which don't really own anything. They aren't assets, only IOUs that the federal government owes back to the trust funds because the federal government has borrowed all the money from those funds and already spent it.

People who are living paycheck to paycheck can't really afford to pay more taxes. But by the same token, there aren't enough super-rich people from whom we can extract all the taxes the country is going to need. And as a result, income taxes are likely going to have to go up dramatically across the board for most Americans—including those in lower-income tax brackets.

Some politicians suggest that we need to charge higher tax rates on corporations and businesses. Unfortunately, businesses don't really pay taxes out of their profits without raising the prices in order to compensate. This means that tax hikes on corporations will just result in more inflation and higher prices for Americans to pay. Businesses simply pass higher taxes on to their customers—American taxpayers.

For many people, paying twice as much in taxes as they're paying now—and maybe even more than that—as a future income tax rate is a reality that they have never considered. And that's on top of inflation, which is an invisible stealth tax—it consumes your spending and waters down the value of your money.

Whether or not wages keep up, most members of the working class aren't going to be able to keep up with inflation, and there are a number of geopolitical elements that are outside of our control.

Wars, supply chain issues, and global shortages can disrupt prices and resources even further.

Shortages can occur for many different reasons, and if we can't quickly offset the problem—by drilling for more oil, for example—the inflation rate is going to remain much higher than it has been in the last two decades.

Consider one of the causes of this inflation: printing too much money! The government printing money in excess to support their spending will most likely devalue the dollar even further. The over-printing of money (U.S. dollars) is a reflection of the U.S. dollar serving as the world's reserve currency, meaning it helps to fuel and prop up the global economy. What a great blessing that is for our country. Or, perhaps, is it a terrible weight around our neck?

The Power of Zero

I often recommend the documentary *The Power of Zero*,[23] which carries themes from David McKnight's book of the same name.[24]

The book and documentary are in line with my views that future tax rates in the United States are going to have to be raised higher and that there is great value in pursuing strategies that can provide a tax rate of zero.

As McKnight tells an audience in the movie, tax rates have historically been much worse—94% during World War II, for example,

---

23 *The Power of Zero*, directed by Doug Orchard, starring David McKnight, David M. Walker, and Maya MacGuineas (United States: Doug Orchard Films, 2018), streaming.

24 David McKnight, *The Power of Zero, Revised and Updated: How to Get to the 0% Tax Bracket and Transform Your Retirement* (New York: Currency, 2018).

and 70% during the 1970s. The current top rate, 37%, isn't so bad by comparison.

So even though people complain that tax rates now are horrible, or the worst they've ever been, they are actually not that bad when compared to other historical periods.

Yet, as David Walker states in the documentary, "The fastest-growing expense in the federal budget is interest on the federal debt. And what do you get from interest on the federal debt? Nothing."

If you have tax-free investments, the government can't raise your taxes.

But there is a caveat to that. The more money you have, the harder it is going to be for you to move all your investments to 100% tax-free. Hence the title of this book, **_Moving to Tax-Free_**—I am trying to help you get as close as you can to tax-free. Unfortunately, some of you might not be able to get all the way there.

But your goal should be to get as close as possible.

The Snake and the Rat

If the Social Security trust fund runs out of money, as projected by the Trustees' report, then by 2033, recipients of Social Security benefits can expect to lose about 22% of their Social Security benefits.[25] Imagine that people who are living on Social Security will have to cut back their annual income by 22% and only live on 78% of what they

---

25 "The 2022 Annual Report of the Board of Trustees of the Federal Old-Age and Survivors Insurance and Federal Disability Insurance Trust Funds," June 2, 2022, https://www.ssa.gov/OACT/TR/2022/tr2022.pdf.

have been promised.

That's if we don't do anything and the dollar remains the reserve currency of the world.

That outcome could have a huge impact on the people who rely on those Social Security payments. Think about your parents, uncles, aunts, or grandparents who are living paycheck to paycheck on the Social Security system having their benefits cut by 22%.

It's a worrisome proposition, especially given that there are 10,000 more baby boomers retiring every day.[26]

The increase in the outflows from the Social Security trust fund is overwhelming. This is all coming to a head as a result of the baby boomers. I'm a baby boomer myself—63 years old. I'm looking forward to being able to claim Medicare, but by the time that I'm ready to do so, we're likely going to be in a big pile of trouble.

Think of a snake that has swallowed a rat. You see this big lump traveling through the snake's body. That big lump is the baby boomers. Now they're reaching retirement age, claiming Medicare benefits, and collecting Social Security benefits. The numbers say our system likely won't be able to sustain the big drawdown from Social Security and Medicare by baby boomers that are coming of age. We are not prepared as a nation for the changes that are going to be required to support and sustain the baby boomers in retirement. Big changes are going to be required, and thus far, politicians have not shown that they are prepared to take the necessary steps to ensure the future of our social insurance programs.

---

26 Jeff Hoyt, "The Baby Boomer Generation," Senior Living, February 28, 2023, https://www.seniorliving.org/life/baby-boomers/.

It is likely that the government will have to limit benefits in some way. Perhaps they won't allow people to claim benefits for Social Security until they reach age 70, because people are living longer. High-income earners will likely have to pay Social Security taxes on their income above the current ceiling ($168,600 as of 2024).[27] Perhaps they will have to pay Social Security on every dollar of income, which would mean that people earning $1 million or more would have to pay a lot more than is currently required. Perhaps the government will even increase the tax rate that is charged on wages for Social Security.

Politicians will likely wait until the last second, just as they have before, to make the draconian changes necessary to address this overwhelming financial mess. The longer they wait, the more desperate the situation will become, as the liabilities will build and build each year we delay addressing this financial catastrophe.

Taxes on Sale (for Now): The Tax Cuts and Jobs Act Sunsets in December 2025

The need to be purposefully strategic becomes more apparent when considering that taxes will soon be rising. We covered some of the bigger-picture reasons why earlier in this chapter.

As I touched on earlier, the Tax Cuts and Jobs Act of 2017 provides for tax rates that are generally 2% to 9% lower than the old tax rates pre-January 2018. That act is scheduled to sunset in December

---

27　Stephen Miller, "2023 Social Security Wage Cap Jumps to $160,200 for Payroll Taxes," Society for HR Management, October 13, 2022, https://www.shrm.org/resourcesandtools/hr-topics/compensation/pages/2023-wage-cap-rises-for-social-security-payroll-taxes.aspx.

2025, meaning that Congress doesn't have to do anything in order for you to experience a tax increase as taxes revert back to the earlier higher rates in the coming years.[28]

The politicians will blame the other side of the aisle for the issue. The government is trying to find money wherever it can, and this is a way to do so without having to hold a vote for a tax increase. Regardless of the makeup of the House, Senate, and Presidency, I don't see the act being extended.

In essence, the current tax rates are **on sale**. This is the discounted price. *Act now and pay the low, low price.* Or you can wait and pay the full government plan price later.

We have no idea what the government may do to the future tax rates. The government will inevitably take their piece of your tax-deferred pie. And their piece can become wider and wider, up to 50% or higher, and you will have no control over the future tax rate. Paying 22% to 24% today is a lot more tolerable than 50%, 60% or even 65% in the future.

If you want to absolutely know how much of your money you can own and keep, your only options are to convert your IRA or 401(k) to a Roth IRA; reposition your taxable money into a permanent cash-value life insurance retirement plan (LIRP); fund a Roth 401(k); or use the other strategies noted in this book.

I want you to have knowledge and certainty about what you own and what is yours—and what will be the government's, as well.

---

28 "Planning for the Tax Cuts and Jobs Act Sunset in 2025," Manning & Napier, January 6, 2023, https://www.manning-napier.com/insights/planning-for-the-tax-cuts-and-jobs-act-sunset-in-2025.

The Challenge

The challenge for people planning for retirement is that we're often living decades longer than our parents did. If someone retires at age 65, they could easily have 20 to 30 years of retirement, and their money has to last that long. What if you beat the averages and live longer?

With inflation consuming your money, you cannot be conservatively invested in bonds with rising interest rates and expect that you're going to stay ahead of a 7% to 9% inflation rate like we experienced in 2022. That's an unrealistic expectation.

Given inflation and rising costs, it's hard enough with the current tax rates to try to just maintain your standard of living. But what will happen when tax rates increase? Not just a little bit but double, as David Walker said will be required.

When our government faces the social insurance dilemma—raising tax rates much higher to support social insurance programs such as Social Security and Medicare, or cutting back programs in order to keep tax rates in check—can you imagine a politician telling a Social Security recipient, "Sorry, but you're going to have to cut your benefits by 22%"? That will not be an easy conversation. Given the choice, I think almost any American will realize that the politicians will take the easy way out and raise our income tax rates to sustain the government's out-of-control spending versus cutting Social Security and Medicare benefits.

Moving to Tax-Free

As all these factors coalesce, any American taxpayer who has not been preparing by moving to tax-free vehicles is bound to get washed over by this impending tsunami of higher tax rates. If taxpayers haven't been preparing, they're going to pay a tremendous price. That tax-deferred 401(k) or that traditional IRA that once looked so attractive because it allowed them to take a tax deduction today and pay the taxes later is going to cost them dearly when the tax bill comes due and their tax rates have doubled or tripled.

As an IRA owner, you can't control what future tax rates are going to be in the United States. You also don't know what your future taxable income will be in a specific future tax year. This is what I am trying to stress to my clients and people I hope to help: because you don't know what your future tax rates will be, you are much better off controlling the tax rate on your tax-deferred accounts by converting those accounts today at tax rates that you know and control, rather than waiting until future tax rates will have to likely double.

Here's an example. Let's say you sell a house or other property, and that forces you into a much higher tax bracket. And then you take your required minimum distribution (RMD) on your IRA, and boom! You'll be taxed at a much higher tax rate.

The 2017 Tax Cuts and Jobs Act opened up a window for you to be strategic and intentional about converting your IRA to a Roth IRA and taking control of what that tax rate will be when you convert.

We use the "tax bracket strategy." We prepare a tax plan for our clients every year. You should prepare a tax plan for yourself too.

Then you can look at the plan and determine, "If I convert $50,000, or $75,000, or $300,000, what tax bracket will that push me into with my other income?" This allows you to be strategic about when and how much you should convert to a Roth IRA in any given year.

As a longtime CERTIFIED FINANCIAL PLANNER™ professional, I see myself as that voice in the wilderness warning taxpayers to begin the process of moving as efficiently and effectively as possible to tax-free vehicles using the tax bracket strategy.

That means not moving too much money in any given year (so you don't have to recognize income in a tax bracket higher than you have planned for) and instead strategically calculating, every year, how much you should be converting and moving from your tax-deferred accounts to a Roth IRA. There, inside of your Roth IRA, your money grows income tax–free and is distributed income tax–free.

Then, as much as the tax code will allow, move your taxable accounts into a tax-free life insurance retirement plan (LIRP) and let your monies grow tax-free in those vehicles.

So, when the time comes and you need that money to live on, you're not getting ravaged by taxes that are going to be out of control and unbelievably worse than they are today.

The disproportionate change of having tax-free accounts versus having taxable accounts in retirement is a must for those people who are planning to retire and want to live comfortably and confidently. Only after you have converted your IRA to a Roth IRA will you know how much of your IRA you own and how much you can truly count on for income in your retirement. Couples who are claiming Social Security benefits will likely have "provisional income," an income calculation used to determine that taxability of your Social Security benefits. (Provisional income includes one half of your Social Security benefits in its calculation.) Married couples with income over $44,000 will have to recognize up to 85% of their Social Security benefits as taxable income.

When, all of a sudden, that is no longer included in taxable income, you just took 85% of your Social Security benefits and moved them to income tax–free income.

That represents a potential tax savings of $11,050 per year for a couple with combined Social Security benefits of $50,000 and taxable income in the 22% federal tax bracket and the same amount in the 4% state income tax bracket.

Here's the math.

Social Security Benefits	$50,000
Taxable Provisional Income (85%)	$42,500
Federal Tax on Provisional Income (22%)	$9,350
State Tax on Provisional Income (*4%)	$1,700

Subject to income tax rates based on your state of residence.
Potential Annual Tax Savings on Social Security Benefits ($9,350 + $1,700) $11,050

Imagine if you could strategically set up the balance of your income to come from tax-free vehicles like Roth IRAs and life insurance retirement plans. You could potentially enjoy tax-free Social Security retirement benefits.

Eliminating or minimizing one of the biggest expenses you're likely to have—income taxes—is a game changer. It can provide you with more after-tax spendable income in retirement. But achieving that outcome requires preparation and focus. It requires you to proceed with strategic intent.

CHAPTER 5

BEGIN WITH THE END IN MIND

Pay Less Taxes over Your Lifetime

"Begin With the End in Mind is based on imagination—the ability to envision in your mind what you cannot at present see with your eyes. It is based on the principle that all things are created twice. There is a mental (first) creation, and a physical (second) creation. The physical creation follows the mental, just as a building follows a blueprint.

"If you don't make a conscious effort to visualize who you are and what you want in life, then you empower other people and circumstances to shape you and your life by default. It's about connecting again with your uniqueness and then defining the personal, moral, and ethical guidelines within which you can most happily express and fulfill yourself."

—STEPHEN R. COVEY[29]

---

29 Stephen Covey, *The 7 Habits of Highly Effective People: 30th Anniversary Edition* (New York, N.Y.: Simon & Schuster, 2020), 113.

What does a successful financial future look like to you?

"Beginning with the end in mind" means making sure that you're putting your ladder against the right wall and climbing with intent. Dr. Stephen R. Covey, through his *7 Habits of Highly Effective People*, notes the importance of picking the right mountain to climb and having that flag and that summit in mind.

That means knowing where you want to go before you start the journey.

Can you imagine making $200,000 a year in retirement and paying *no federal or state income taxes*? And whatever is leftover for your children is income tax–free as well.

That vision might feel like a pipe dream right now, but it's not; it's possible.

Moving to tax-free is the intentional and deliberate strategic repositioning of your assets and income sources to investment vehicles that provide income that is tax-free (tax-exempt) from federal and state income taxes and is not includable in provisional income. The provisional income calculation determines the taxability of your Social Security benefits, and it can also have a dramatic impact on how close you can get to living completely tax-free.

Planning ahead means:

- *Strategically arranging your income sources so that your Social Security benefits are income tax–free.*
- *Using the tax laws to keep your taxable income as low as possible while still helping you achieve your charitable giving and legacy goals income-tax-free and estate-tax-free, while still maintaining*

> *your quality of life and standard of living goals.*
> - *Using all your assets in a comprehensive tax-reduction strategy to produce tax-free income, avoid estate taxation, and create the most beneficial tax outcome possible for you and your family, leaving a tax-free legacy where possible.*

While you are working, your wages are taxed as ordinary income, and it is exceedingly difficult to legally avoid paying income tax on that type of income. (Doing so could get you in lots of trouble.)

On the other hand, once you retire, we can control which bucket your income is coming from (which retirement income bucket you are pulling income from), and, if we have planned properly, that income can come from sources that generate tax-free income.

The Tax-Free Retirement (or as Close as We Can Get)

You may not be able to get all the way to zero taxable income.

You most likely will have some earned income in retirement from business enterprises, real estate, or other passive income sources that you have not been able to convert to tax-free income sources.

Our goal is to try to keep your Social Security benefits income tax–free. We can do that if all your other income is tax-free income when it comes to federal and state income tax laws.

If you or a spouse have a pension from work that pays retirement income, for example, it is going to be nearly impossible to keep your Social Security benefits free from taxation.

If you have other sources that generate income in retirement (rental real estate income, business income, etc.), these sources may also make your Social Security benefits taxable because your income will not be able to stay below the prescribed limits that determine if your Social Security will be taxed.

Ideally, when you have completed your move to tax-free, you could have all the income you desire from tax-free sources, and your Social Security benefits would still not be subject to federal or state income tax.

But reaching that tax-free retirement—or something close to it—requires you to begin moving as much as you reasonably can to tax-free vehicles sooner rather than later. That means strategically creating a tax plan each year, planning how much you can begin moving from taxable and tax-deferred investment vehicles to sheltered tax-free investment vehicles.

This effort comes at a price. You will generally have to recognize taxable income in the short term as you move from a taxable or tax-deferred bucket to a tax-free bucket. But you will likely wind up paying a lot less now than you would have to pay in the future when we have higher tax rates.

Avoiding a MEC (Modified Endowment Contract) Mess

Sometimes I meet with prospects who want to move their money to tax-free all at once. With our current tax laws, the IRS has purposely set it up so that you can't really do that without being punished, both on tax-deferred monies and on taxable monies.

If someone tries to convert their whole IRA to a Roth IRA all at once, they will force their effective tax rate on all that money into the highest tax bracket. For example, if somebody has a $3 million IRA and they want to convert all $3 million of it, the highest tax rate right now is 37%.[30] They're going to be subject to that 37% tax rate on almost all that Roth IRA conversion.

The same thing applies to life insurance when we're moving taxable money. These are monies that have already been taxed but are subject to capital gains tax and ordinary income tax on most interest and dividends. Suppose we're trying to move taxable funds into a LIRP (a tax-free cash-value permanent life insurance policy to be used in retirement). You will see in the financial services industry that some professionals don't really care about a client benefiting from tax-free income in retirement. They'll agree to take all $3 million and say, "Yes, let's put all of this in a life insurance policy right now."

Now, if you're just leaving that policy for a death benefit, that works out fine because the death benefit remains tax-free. But if you want to borrow against that policy and use the income tax–free benefits for retirement income? That will not work. When you fully fund a permanent cash-value life insurance policy up front in the first year, the Internal Revenue Code requires that the life insurance policy gets changed into a "MEC," which stands for modified endowment contract.[31]

If a life insurance policy owner overfunds a life insurance policy

---

30 Sarah Foster, "2022–2023 Tax Brackets and Federal Income Tax Rates," Bankrate, January 17, 2023, https://www.bankrate.com/taxes/tax-brackets/#tax-bracket-2022.

31 Akhilesh Ganti, "Modified Endowment Contract (MEC): Definition and Tax Implication," Investopedia, last updated May 11, 2022, https://www.investopedia.com/terms/m/modified-endowment-contract.asp.

with too much premium the first year, or at any time too early in the policy, you will force it to become a modified endowment contract. By paying the insurance company too much premium sooner than planned on the life insurance illustration, you have caused the policy to blow up.

You've basically just turned that life insurance policy into an annuity—so any growth on that policy, if you go to take it out, is included as taxable income, taxed at ordinary income rates.

You need to treat a LIRP similarly to a Roth conversion, where you're paying premiums in over a number of years, so you don't modify that contract and "MEC" it by investing too much money into the policy too soon.

Insurance companies will use software to calculate what those limits are. And you can fund it quicker, maybe over four or five years instead of over 10 or 20. But you have to be careful with that.

People come to us worried about the tax rates, wanting to make things happen right away, and I often share the previous example of an orchard or vineyard. The farmer has to invest the time, effort, patience, and diligence to wait for their crop to mature, and they have to water and weed and fertilize it over a number of years. It's the same thing with moving to tax-free—it's a process, and you can't just do it all at once. Otherwise, you're penalized.

The sooner people can start their move to tax-free, the further along they can get in the process.

They have to remain patient, dedicated, and persistent in repositioning their monies every year. Moving them to their permanent cash-value life insurance policies. Preparing the tax and financial planning in order to know how much they should be repositioning and funding into that life insurance policy every year. It really requires a lot of strategic intent, gumption, and commitment to make this move.

Push It to the Limit

Did you know that the IRS has created limits on the amount of money you can invest into a permanent cash-value life insurance policy?

If the IRS limits how much money you can put into a cash-value life insurance policy, it might be a good thing to invest money into a tax-free life insurance policy, right?

If the IRS limits something, you typically want to use up the maximum amount that the IRS will allow you to use. If you put in the maximum limit without making the contract a modified endowment contract, then you will have the ability to borrow from the policy, and those loan proceeds are tax-free. By not making the mistake of forcing that life insurance policy to become a modified endowment contract, you can receive all the tax-free benefits that life insurance has to offer, as living benefits to the policy owner and their family instead of waiting for the death benefit of that policy.

Insurance companies are very attuned to this. So, if somebody sends in too much premium, they will almost always reach out and contact the policyholder and warn them.

You have to be careful that you don't get too exuberant and just send in money to the insurance company, thinking that you can add more money at any time. The funds the insurance company loans to you are not your funds. Your funds remain invested and earn a potential return on the strategy they are invested in. The insurance company loans you funds from their general account and will charge you an interest rate, say as an example 4%. Your investments can earn more or less than this amount. Since many of them historically have earned more (i.e., 6%), this can give you the potential to benefit from the arbitrage on the difference (6% – 4% = 2%).

Making the Move More Manageable

The move to tax-free is easier and more manageable with moderate savings in the $200,000 to $500,000 range. Someone could handle that process over the course of a few years without blowing up their tax rate. If you have a big retirement plan with $1 million, $10 million, or more, though, it's going to be harder for you to get there, and it will require more tax and financial planning.

The more money you wish to move to tax-free vehicles, the more your efforts need to be deliberate, making smart use of the effective tax rates.

People in that lower savings tier have a higher likelihood of achieving a tax-free retirement by avoiding getting their Social Security benefits taxed.

Buckets of Money

One of your most important planning steps in setting up your tax-free retirement is making sure you're structuring your accounts in a diversified manner.

Diversification is a popular strategy in finance. There's the diversification that someone worries about when they manage their investments. We don't always know what asset class is going to perform best and what's going to perform worse, so by spreading out your assets across multiple asset classes, you might get a little scraped up here and there, but you're not going to get killed by a slide in any one asset class.

Through diversification, you have enough non-correlated asset classes included in your portfolio that if two or three of them are going down, you have another two or three that are either holding their own or going up in value.

We don't have to be invested in all asset classes, but we should be diversified in enough of them so they're not correlated. If you think of two roller coasters racing on parallel tracks, you don't want them both going down at the same time—if one is going down, the other one should be going up, so the average is consistent.

Diversification is a way to cut down on volatility. Case in point is the S&P 500, which was down 15%–22% during most of 2022,[32] while energy companies were up about 60% during the year.[33] So, if you invested some in the S&P 500 and some in energy, you could offset parts of your portfolio that are going down or sideways with other allocations that are increasing in value.

---

32 "S&P 500 Index," *Wall Street Journal*, accessed May 1, 2023, https://www.wsj.com/market-data/quotes/index/SPX/advanced-chart.

33 Shrilekha Pethe, "7 Best Energy Stocks to Buy Now," Kiplinger, last updated April 3, 2023, https://www.kiplinger.com/investing/stocks/best-energy-stocks.

With retirement planning, you're looking for a combination of buckets that you can choose to pull retirement income from. Using the right combination from different buckets in any given year can potentially give you choices and help you navigate the retirement minefield with success.

For example, if and when the equity (stock) markets are down in the future, you can pull equity out of your house with a reverse mortgage and use those loan proceeds as tax-free retirement income. And then, when the equity markets recover and go back up, you can take the proceeds out of your stock market portfolio and pay back into your reverse mortgage line of credit, while picking up a mortgage interest deduction along the way.

Perhaps you've got a certain amount of money in a Roth IRA. You want to figure out how much to take out of your traditional IRA and how much to take out of your Roth IRA so that you don't make your Social Security benefits taxable, or at least keep them less taxable.

The goal is to have and use different buckets of money with different tax treatments in such a combination that it provides the best tax-free benefit for you in retirement. Some of these tax-free vehicles are more advantageous than others, but you're moving from taxable to tax-free, so your retirement is much more favorable—your money is diversified in such a way that you can pick different buckets of your money that you can pull from on an annual basis.

The Importance of Objectivity

If we're in the go-go years and the market is going up, people are inclined to take more risks.

When the market is down, people become more conservative. They don't want to lose money, and they want to protect what they have. The fear spectrum goes up and down depending on the economy, markets and their movements up and down, geopolitical situations playing out around the world, war, inflation, recessions, and our own government's actions or failures to act to address our problems.

The benefit financial and tax advisors bring to the equation is objectivity. It's not our money. We are much less inclined to make emotionally based decisions because of our training and experience.

We can look at your investments from a distance and see if they're being invested too conservatively or too aggressively compared to your risk tolerance. We help you create investment plans that will be advantageous for you based on your specific needs and situation.

We're focused on sequence of return risk—ensuring that people are protecting their income sources during the early years of retirement. With dips in the market, you can let your long-term investment remain invested (that's money you won't need for 10 years or more), and you'll give those long-term investments a chance to recover without affecting your income needs in the near term.

Avoiding the Potholes

Some clients seek a financial advisor when they're starting to approach retirement. As they reach age 55 and older, they want to see if they're on track. Many appreciate a second set of eyes on their retirement plan. Others are ready to retire or are close to retirement; they've been working with an advisor, but they aren't happy with their advisor or the quality of the advice and services they are receiving.

The bells and alarms start going off, blaring. Their risk tolerance doesn't match the way their money is invested. *I never intended to lose so much money.* They were making money in the good times, but the advisor kept riding that horse full tilt and didn't do anything to protect the client and adjust the portfolio during the lean times.

This reinforces the need for active financial management. The way I describe it to clients is by asking them to imagine we're driving down the freeway. In Arizona, we have four or five lanes across the freeway, and the speed limit is 65, but everyone drives 75 to 80 miles per hour because it's flat and straight.

If I'm driving in the center lane and I'm looking ahead and I see a pothole, you'd expect me to change lanes and avoid the pothole. Similarly, as a financial advisor, I'm looking at the financial potholes ahead and trying to do everything I can to avoid them for my clients.

A lot of planners are focused on "staying the course."

We believe our financial and tax planning, proactive investment management, and ongoing forward-looking wealth management set us apart and differentiate us from most other financial advisors.

We might not be able to drive around all the potholes. But we can avoid the big ones, and that can make a big difference for our clients.

Be Purposefully Strategic

One of my personal mottos is to **"live my life with strategic intent."** I do not want to allow life to happen to me by accident. I want to act with purpose and take intentional actions to achieve my life goals.

There is so much in this life that's out of our control. But we can act—right now, here, today—on the things that are within our control. I invite you to be intentional about the income tax rates you will pay over your remaining life (the tax rates you will have to pay on your IRA and other tax-deferred assets) and to be intentional as to when you will choose to pay the taxes that will inevitably come due on your IRA and 401(k).

So many people think about retirement planning in terms of the future. *It can wait; I'm only in my thirties or forties. This doesn't apply to me yet. I'm just paying my taxes every year.*

But there is so much you can do now to prepare for your future. You could start putting away some money every year into a Roth IRA, for example. That is living with strategic intent.

This reminds me of the Aesop fable "The Ant and the Grasshopper." While the ants spend the summer working, drying out grain for the winter ahead, the grasshopper spends his time making music. Needless to say, the fall comes, and the starving grasshopper shows up with his fiddle under his arm, humbly begging the ants for a bite to eat.

Where your retirement planning is concerned, be the ant, and start putting money aside while the sun is shining. Instead of doing it all at once, diligently save all summer long. Live your life with strategic intent—start now.

Tax Bracket Strategy

Again, the goal here is strategic intent—being deliberate about your approach.

I'm not talking about converting your IRA to a Roth in a willy-nilly fashion. I am talking about strategically planning and purposefully calculating your tax bracket, each and every year.

Some people in the industry call this using "**the tax bracket strategy**." Ideally, what we are trying to do is to persuade you to convert the right amount of your IRA to a Roth IRA each and every year. You will recognize the income and pay the tax *while taxes are still on sale.*

Different income levels come with different tax rates.

The chart on the next page shows the 2024 federal income tax rates for single filers and married individuals filing jointly. The tax brackets represent different levels of taxable income, not adjusted gross income. Remember, your taxable income is not determined until after your itemized deductions or standard deduction are subtracted from your adjusted gross income.

Your taxable income is then used to calculate how much tax you will owe.

The federal tax rate moves from 10% to 12% to 22% to 24% to 32% to 35%, and it tops off at 37%. Some of those jumps aren't very big—22% to 24%, for example. But 24% to 32% is a big spike. That's an 8% jump in marginal tax rate.

For a single filer in the 24% tax bracket, let's say that you're making $100,000 a year and you have an IRA or a 401(k) that you can start converting to Roth. You could convert another $70,000 and use up the rest of that 24% tax bracket without jumping into the next higher 32% marginal tax bracket.

KEY NUMBERS FOR 2024

TAX BRACKET

TAXABLE INCOME BETWEEN:

SINGLE

$0—$11,600	10%
$11,601—$47,150	12%
$47,151—$100,525	22%
$100,526—$191,950	24%
$191,951—$243,725	32%
$243,726—$609,350	35%
$609,351+	37%

MARRIED, FILING JOINTLY

$0—$23,200	10%
$23,201—$94,300	12%
$94,301—$201,050	22%
$201,051—$383,900	24%
$383,901—$487,450	32%
$487,451—$731,200	35%
$731,201+	37%

This strategy is much easier said than done. I cannot tell you how many times I have helped clients plan to move to tax-free, only to have them swallow hard when they see how much they will pay in taxes the first year they begin this strategy.

Instead of focusing on the dollar amount, they should instead focus on the percentage of tax they have to pay.

We have two tax rates in the United States that we need to pay attention to. The first is your **marginal tax rate**, and the second is your **effective tax rate**. Your marginal tax rate is the percentage of tax you will have to pay on the next dollar that you earn or have to recognize as taxable income.

Your effective tax rate is your actual tax rate—the rate of tax that you actually pay, after deductions, adjustments, and tax credits. It is the effective tax rate that is the actual rate of tax you pay on your taxable income.[34]

With our 24% tax bracket example, with marginal tax brackets, you can actually cross into the 32% bracket *a little bit* without it raising your taxes too much—once you cross into the next higher tax bracket, the next dollar earned is taxed at the higher marginal rate. Early dollars, in comparison, will be taxed at the lower rates of 10%, 12%, and 22% sequentially as your income adds up for the year. So, if you can keep the effective tax rate in the 19% to 24% range, you're in pretty good shape. And then you can convert money year by year and systematically use the tax bracket strategy over a number of years.

---

34 Hana LaRock, "Marginal vs. Effective Tax Rate: What's the Difference?," Bankrate, February 27, 2023, https://www.bankrate.com/taxes/marginal-vs-effective-tax-rate.

If you pay attention to the effective tax rate you will pay as a percentage rather than focusing on the amount of tax dollars, it makes it much easier for you to consider converting your IRA to a tax-free Roth IRA.

When you see the difference in the percentage of the marginal tax bracket versus your effective tax bracket, it will help you realize just how huge the sale on tax rates currently is.

If you can lock in the lower tax rates and convert your money now—before the Tax Cuts and Jobs Act of 2017 sunsets—you're going to wind up paying a lower tax rate on your IRA to Roth IRA conversion than you will in 2026 and the years that follow.

The goal is to convert as much money as you can now using the tax bracket strategy. To be guided by strategic intent and purpose. To have the destination in mind before starting your journey of moving to tax-free.

CHAPTER 6

CONVENTIONAL WISDOM—THE TAX-DEFERRED PARADIGM TRAP

Conquering the Deadly Ds

"We have met the enemy and he is us."

—WALT KELLY[35]

*L*et's talk about marshmallows.

In the early 1970s, a Stanford University professor conducted a study about delayed gratification. In the study, preschool-aged children were given a choice: they could have one marshmallow right away, or if they could wait and forgo immediate gratification, they could receive two marshmallows.[36] In other words, if they waited a few more minutes to eat the first marshmallow, they were rewarded with a second marshmallow for being willing to wait.

---

35 "We Have Met the Enemy and He Is Us," Ohio State University, accessed May 1, 2023, https://library.osu.edu/site/40stories/2020/01/05/we-have-met-the-enemy/.

36 Janine Zacharia, "The Bing 'Marshmallow Studies': 50 Years of Continuing Research," Stanford School of Humanities and Sciences, September 24, 2015, https://bingschool. stanford.edu/news/bing-marshmallow-studies-50-years-continuing-research.

Some of the children immediately grabbed the marshmallow.

The ones who waited distracted themselves or sang to pass the time, while others whispered affirmative statements.

The "Marshmallow Test" revealed a lot about the willpower required to overcome impatience and the self-control required to be able to enjoy the benefits of delayed gratification. In recent years, a restaging of the study has suggested that children's affluence and economic background contributed to their ability to hold out for another marshmallow.[37]

Think about paying your own taxes and the delayed gratification that might be required in terms of the Marshmallow Test. The tax industry has taught the American taxpayer to immediately take the marshmallow—we are all so focused on lowering this year's tax payments and maximizing our current tax refund instead of considering the benefits of taking a much longer-term view of what may be possible.

Many tax accountants and financial professionals push three misguided strategies. They instruct you to:

1. delay,

2. deduct, or

3. defer

your tax payment to Uncle Sam as long as possible. Everything

---

37 Tyler Watts, Greg Duncan, and Haonan Quan, "Revisiting the Marshmallow Test: A Conceptual Replication Investigating Links Between Early Delay of Gratification and Later Outcomes," *Psychological Science* 29, no. 7 (2018): 1159–77, https://doi. org/10.1177/0956797618761661.

to them is all about *the current tax year*, when instead they should be helping you focus on **lowering income taxes over your lifetime**.

The Deadly Ds

Taxpayers share much of the responsibility for this shortsighted approach to tax planning and tax preparation because they ask the wrong questions.

- How much will I have to pay this year?
- How much is my tax refund?
- Is there anything I can do to pay less tax this year?

Those questions are shortsighted. Americans have trained their tax professionals to only focus on the here and now. They have not had incentive, experience, or training in how to look ahead over the next 5, 10, 20, or even 30 years to help you figure out how you can lower your lifetime tax obligations.

The assumption that many tax professionals make is that tax rates will remain level at the current rates we enjoy today. They are only worried about this year, or maybe next year. They have not been trained to worry about tax planning for the remainder of your life.

This reminds me of the Mervyn's department store TV commercials from back in the day, showing the woman at the door pleading, "Open, open, open…" But this time, the customer is at the door of their tax professional's office, and they're saying, "Refund, refund, refund."

They want to know how big their tax refund will be. The whole industry is built around helping people find tax deductions for the current tax year. Nobody is looking down the road into the future. Delaying, deferring, and deducting everything you can this year may not really be in your best interest.

It's so very easy to fall into the trap of focusing on what's directly ahead of you, especially with the average tax refund in 2022 totaling more than $3,000.[38] People can choose to do a lot of things with $3,000.

With tax rates poised to keep rising, that hefty tax refund you collect this year could cost you mightily in the years ahead. Here is what conventional wisdom teaches about **delay**, **deduct**, and **defer** and how you can conquer the Deadly Ds.

Delay

Many taxpayers look for any chance they can get to delay paying their taxes. But those tax-deferred taxes don't go away, and when the time comes for taxpayers to retire and withdraw the money, the tax bill comes due.

The most notable example of delaying paying taxes is IRA and 401(k) contributions, where you delay paying taxes on that money until retirement or later when the RMD rules will require you to take the money out and pay the taxes at that time. At that point, you will have to pay the taxes at the future income tax rate, which will likely be much higher than today's current tax rates.

---

38 Maurie Backman, "The Average Tax Refund for 2022 Keeps Growing. How Does Yours Stack Up?," The Ascent, June 9, 2022, https://www.fool.com/the-ascent/taxes/articles/the-average-tax-refund-for-2022-keeps-growing-how-does-yours-stack-up/.

Americans' 401(k) savings rate in 2022 reached its highest point in recent memory. People are interested in setting money aside for the future. But many of those with 401(k) accounts probably haven't thought much about the tax burden they will face in the next decade or two.

You may not be able to control the future tax year in which you will have to pay the tax on your 401(k) nor the tax rate in that future year. Someday in the future, you will be forced to recognize the income and pay the tax, either due to RMDs, or because you need the income, or because your spouse or children were forced to take it out and pay the taxes on it.

Deduct

Of course, we want to deduct everything we possibly can from our taxable income. Who wouldn't want to deduct everything they legally can? There are so many different deductions you can claim (and I would suggest that you do so, if the deductions are applicable):

- Mortgage interest on your primary home
- State income and sales tax paid
- Medical expenses and medical insurance premiums
- Charitable donations to your beloved charities

The deductions you should avoid come from purposefully choosing to not take an available *tax deduction* in the current year. I would rather you pay the tax now so that the growth going forward is growing income tax–free from both federal and state income tax.

That means purposefully choosing not to take an IRA deduction and instead choosing to fund a nondeductible Roth IRA contribution, or perhaps instead of taking a deduction for your 401(k) contribution, electing to contribute to and fund your Roth 401(k) at work.

Defer

"Deferring" means putting off paying taxes until you need the money in retirement—which means a tax cancer could be growing on your IRA account for many years. As we've noted, future income tax rates are likely going to be much higher than what they are today. With tax-deferred retirement saving plans, you are at the mercy of the future tax rate.

Many tax professionals recommend deferring taxes. They will tell you it is the best tax plan. The questions that you should consider asking about deferring taxes include:

- If I defer taxes now, how long will the tax obligation be deferred?
- When will I have to pay the tax?
- What will the future tax rate be when I have to pay the tax?
- How much other income will I have in that future tax year that might push me into a higher tax bracket?

You see, it is not clear cut. The questions are important to consider, and the answers are complex. The solutions require a complete understanding of your potential short-term and long-term tax and financial situation.

With a fiscal tax storm brewing, it's time to act. Right now. Today.

The Next Best Thing—with a Catch

Tax deferral is the next best thing to tax-free. Some tax-deferred vehicles are extremely viable, and we use and recommend them when appropriate:

- Long-term capital gains, for assets held for more than one year
- 1031 exchanges on real estate transactions
- Funding tax-deferred retirement accounts like IRAs, 401(k)s, and tax-deferred annuities
- 529 education plans

The key to using these tax-deferred vehicles is that you need to know how they work in combination with the rest of your tax planning, retirement accounts, and other investment vehicles.

For some people, delaying income into retirement could make their Social Security taxable, which could be incredibly significant for their total tax situation. Imagine the difference between receiving $40,000 a year of Social Security benefits income tax–free, versus adding that on top of other taxable income, only to go from zero tax to a 20% or 30% tax rate. Falling off a tax cliff can be painfully expensive.[39]

Conquering the Deadly Ds

Instead of worrying about how much money you'll pay in taxes this

---

39 Jim Tankersley, "Republicans, Eyeing Majority, Float Changes to Social Security and Medicare," *New York Times*, November 2, 2022, https://www.nytimes.com/2022/11/02/us/politics/republicans-social-security-medicare.html.

year, the question you should ask is, "How much money will I pay in taxes over my remaining lifetime?"

Instant gratification using the Deadly Ds will deprive you of a tax-free future, which could make a dramatic difference for your financial outlook as tax rates go higher and higher.

You can conquer the Deadly Ds by informing yourself and asking the right questions. It's tempting to seek a big tax refund, to reach for the marshmallow, but the rewards of delayed gratification are worth the wait. Believe me, it will be well worth it.

CHAPTER 7

TAX-FREE—WHAT DOES THAT REALLY MEAN?

In Order to Truly Be Tax-Free, Income Must Meet These Four Criteria

"The journey to financial freedom starts the MINUTE you decide you were destined for prosperity, not scarcity—for abundance, not lack."

—MARK VICTOR HANSEN[40]

L et's dive into what moving to tax-free really means.

As I noted earlier, in the tax code, there's no such thing as tax-free—the exact IRS term is *"tax-exempt"*—but that term alone doesn't describe the full scope and benefits of moving to tax-free.

In order to qualify for my definition of tax-free, income must meet four criteria:

---

40 Mark Victor Hansen, *The One Minute Millionaire: The Enlightened Way to Wealth* (New York: Currency, 2002), xi.

1. The income has to be free from being subject to federal income taxes.

2. The income has to be free from being subject to state income taxes.

3. The income must not trigger provisional income on your Social Security benefits.

4. The income must not add to your adjusted gross income, making more of your capital gains income taxable.

You may not be able to get completely moved over to tax-free income, but moving in the direction of tax-free will keep you from going over a tax cliff as you approach or reach retirement.

Let's break down these four criteria further.

1. The income has to be free from being subject to federal income taxes.

Two of the primary vehicles that you can use to generate tax-free income are:

- the Roth IRA (Roth 401(k)), and
- the LIRP.

You can receive several hundred thousand dollars of income from these vehicles each year and pay zero income tax on your Social Security benefits and zero federal and state income taxes.

There are other possible sources of tax-free income as well. With an HSA, you can potentially get a state tax deduction on the front end, and if you use it for medical expenses, that spending is not includable in federal or state taxable income—therefore, it becomes a tax-free distribution.

2. The income has to be free from being subject to state income taxes.

A handful of states don't tax your retirement income. If you are lucky enough to live in one of those states, great! There are currently eight states without a state income tax: Alaska, Florida, Nevada, South Dakota, Tennessee, Texas, Washington, and Wyoming.

It used to be easier for high-income earners to write off all their state taxes, but it's much tougher to do that now.

Where we used to see taxpayers deduct their mortgage interest on their primary residence and write the interest off for their state and local taxes, seniors age 62 and older, if they have a mortgage, can put the balance on a reverse mortgage. Maybe they won't pay on it for a few years—the interest builds up, and then selectively, in a given year, they will pay the mortgage down, pay all that interest, and receive a big mortgage interest deduction. They can then use that deduction to offset making a Roth conversion.

Similarly, with college 529 plans, grandparents or other relatives can contribute funds for their grandchildren and, in some states, including Arizona, receive a state tax deduction.

The Tax Cuts and Jobs Act of 2017 restricted or eliminated many itemized deductions, making state tax deductions all the more valuable. On your federal return, you can only deduct medical expenses that exceeded 7.5% of your adjusted gross income in 2022.[41] In Arizona, on the other hand, you can write off 100% of medical expenses against state income taxes, so we encourage our clients to give us all of their costs associated with medical expenses, including dental work, glasses, hearing aids, and doctor's visits each year.[42]

3. The income must not trigger provisional income on your Social Security benefits.

Provisional income includes all your taxable income, including wages, taxable and tax-exempt municipal bond interest, capital gains, dividends, pensions, self-employment, and retirement income. Provisional income also includes one half of your Social Security benefits.

If you are able to arrange your financial affairs so that you can keep your taxable income low enough that your Social Security benefits are not includable in taxable income, that becomes a huge tax-free pay raise.

The concept of controlling your provisional income is foundational to the opportunity to move as close to tax-free as you can. Structuring your affairs so that your Social Security benefits are income tax–free should be one of your primary goals.

The calculation for provisional income has not been adjusted for inflation for decades, so a married couple filing jointly with less than $32,000 of provisional income ($25,000 for single filers) will have

---

41 Jim Probasco, "Tax Deductions That Went Away with the Tax Cuts and Jobs Act," Investopedia, last updated February 24, 2023, https://www.investopedia.com/tax-deductions-that-are-going-away-4582165.

42 "Tax Conformity FAQs," Arizona Department of Revenue, accessed May 1, 2023, https://azdor.gov/individual-income-tax-filing-assistance/tax-conformity-faqs.

no taxable Social Security benefits.[43]

For couples with provisional income from $32,000 to $44,000, 50% of their benefits will be includable in taxable income ($25,000 to $34,000 for single filers).

If your provisional income is above $44,000 for married couples and $34,000 for single filers, as much as 85% of your Social Security is now included in taxable income.

All other taxable income is included in that calculation—even municipal bond interest, which is not taxable for federal tax purposes and may or may not be tax-free for state taxes, depending on your municipality and the bond you're investing in.

If you have too much municipal bond interest, it can force your Social Security (which would have otherwise been income tax–free) to become subject to federal and state income taxes.

4. The income must not add to your adjusted gross income, making more of your capital gains income taxable.

Some investments have consequences. It's best to minimize or offset your exposure to capital gains taxes, which are triggered when you sell assets such as stocks and bonds, and possibly even your home, depending on the value realized and how long you've owned it.

---

43 Christy Bieber, "Despite Big Social Security Changes in 2022, This Rule Will Stay the Same—and It Could Cost You," The Motley Fool, December 14, 2021, https://www.fool.com/investing/2021/12/14/this-social-security-rule-could-cost-you/.

Adding to your adjusted gross income can push your other capital gains and ordinary income into a higher tax bracket. You can also offset capital gains with capital losses—using investment losses to keep your AGI in check.

This is important, given that the long-term capital gains tax rates in 2024 are 0%, 15%, or 20%, depending on your taxable income.[44]

Roth IRAs and LIRPs are not subject to capital gains taxes.

You should also try to minimize or avoid alternative minimum tax and net investment income tax, or NIIT, which should not be included in the calculation affecting your adjusted gross income. Tax-free income should not push up either of these ancillary taxes.

Defining the Stakes

In 2015, the Social Security Administration ran projections suggesting that 56% of recipients will owe federal income tax on at least part of their benefit income in the coming decades.[45] Among those who owe taxes on their benefits, the median share of benefits owed as tax was estimated at 12% in the coming decades.

Following this path will cost some people a lot of money. But luckily for you, it doesn't have to be that way.

---

44 Jason Fernando, "Capital Gains Tax: What It Is, How It Works, and Current Rates," Investopedia, last updated March 31, 2023, https://www.investopedia.com/terms/c/capital_gains_tax.asp.

45 Patrick Purcell, "Income Taxes on Social Security Benefits," Social Security Office of Retirement and Disability Policy, December 2015, https://www.ssa.gov/policy/docs/issuepapers/ip2015-02.html.

The Ideal Place to Be

Let's consider my hypothetical couple Bill and Sally who are poster children for moving to tax-free.

They have been high earners over the years. They are on an aggressive plan of converting their IRAs to Roth IRAs. They are also moving their taxable money into a separate LIRP for each of them. We are moving the funds to the LIRPs over the next four years.

Before converting their IRA money to Roth IRAs, they would have been in line for a hefty tax burden on their benefits. But now, they can expect yearly tax-free income from each of their Roth IRAs and tax-free income from each of their LIRPs. Combined, those income streams should be about $145,000 per year. (Example of the math: $3.6 M in the tax-free Roth IRAs and tax-free LIRP accounts providing a tax-free income stream of 4% annually before SSA benefits = $144,822.92.) They expect their Social Security benefits to be $60,000 per year combined when they claim them. So, they will enjoy no taxes on their Roth IRA distributions and no taxes on their life insurance retirement plan income either. Imagine having $200,000 tax-free spendable income each year without any income tax drag. No federal income taxes due, and no state income taxes due, and no taxes on their Social Security benefits either.

That is an ideal place for anyone.

Obviously, the move to tax-free isn't all-encompassing. Pensions, for example, always represent taxable income, taxed at ordinary income rates. That truth makes these strategies even more important—the pension payments, when combined with your Social Security benefits, make it more likely that you'll trigger taxability of your Social Security benefits under the provisional income calculation, and will probably be includable in taxable income to the point where 85% of your Social Security benefits will now be included in your taxable income.

Triggering that top tier for provisional income puts you over the edge of a tax cliff. If a couple's annual income triggers taxability of their Social Security benefits of $44,001, it can cost them $10,098 in federal and state taxes, just like that.[46] And that's with a tax rate of just 22% for federal taxes and 5% for state income taxes.

Moving to Tax-Free Takes Time—Literally Years

Let's circle back to the story of Bill and Sally, the poster children. Did you notice how we are moving money over to tax-free vehicles over four years?

Moving to tax-free takes time, and it requires a strategic process to take advantage of the opportunities that are afforded to you as an American taxpayer. This is not something that you can just do overnight.

Certainly, you can pay all the taxes up front, pushing yourself into a higher tax bracket, and that will lock in the tax rate that you will pay on all your Roth conversion.

---

46 Julia Kagan, "Provisional Taxes: What They Are and How They Work," Investopedia, last updated October 8, 2022, https://www.investopedia.com/terms/p/provisional-income.asp.

But moving your taxable money (money that's not in tax-deferred accounts like traditional IRAs and 401(k)s) is strategically and systematically repositioned to a cash-value life insurance policy. Funding a cash-value life insurance policy retirement plan generally takes somewhere between 4 and 20 years.

If you try to overfund one of these programs, it could backfire on you and become very expensive. So, moving to tax-free is a strategic initiative that requires time, planning, commitment, and dedication in order to achieve your goals.

Think of it this way: If the IRS is limiting the amount of money that you can put into an investment (say permanent cash-value life insurance), do you think that it's in your best interest, or the government's, to fund such an account?

Avoiding a Future Panic

There was a *panic* in the summer and fall of 2021 after President Joe Biden proposed a new capital gains tax rate of 39.6%. At the time, the long-term capital gains rate was only 20%.[47] People were desperate to sell real estate and businesses ahead of the new higher rate.

That proposed tax rate was later chipped away, but it reinforced an important point: **You have no control over when, or by how much, future tax rates may change**. Who knows who will be in control of our government when you need to take income from your retirement accounts?

---

47 Kelley R. Taylor, "Biden Calls for Doubling of Capital Gains Tax Rate," Kiplinger, last updated March 10, 2023, https://www.kiplinger.com/taxes/biden-calls-for-doubling-capital-gains-tax-rate.

And how will you be able to control what tax rate you will pay in retirement?

You won't…unless you move to tax-free and lock in the tax rate you will pay today. Doing so will help you avoid the cancer that is deferred taxes—and one of the primary weapons in moving to tax-free is the IRA conversion to a Roth IRA.

CHAPTER 8

WHAT PROCESS SHOULD I USE TO CONVERT TO A ROTH IRA?

The Money in Your Roth IRA is the Most Sacred Money You Have

"Tax-free money always grows the fastest, because it's never eroded by future taxes."

—ED SLOTT[48]

The money in your Roth IRA is the most sacred money you have.

It is the *last* money that you should touch if you can help it. The goal with a Roth IRA is to let the money in your Roth account grow as long as possible because that growth is tax-free for both federal and state taxes. Pulling money out of your Roth IRA account prematurely will only diminish the account's potential long-term re-

---

48 Lorie Konish, "Why It's 'Just No Question' New Investors Should Start By Opening a Roth IRA, Expert Says," CNBC, last updated May 24, 2023, https://www.cnbc.com/2023/04/21/its-no-question-new-investors-should-open-a-roth-ira-expert-says.html.

turn and could incur potential penalty fees and taxes.

The exception is if we need to pull income from your Roth IRA in combination with other investment and retirement accounts to provide you with the most tax-efficient retirement income plan possible for that year.

Roth IRAs were established through the Taxpayer Relief Act of 1997.[49] They are named after Senator William V. Roth Jr. from Delaware, who was chairman of the Senate Finance Committee—he sponsored the legislation behind the account.[50]

A quarter century after they first became available, Roth IRAs are held by more than 25 million households, roughly one-fifth of U.S. households.[51] But many people remain confused about Roth IRAs.[52] And, as a result, they could be missing out on a great opportunity to plan for their future.

Roth IRA Benefits

Some of the benefits of the Roth IRA conversion include the fact that there's no income limitation for how much you can earn in the tax year that you convert your traditional IRA to a Roth IRA. Additionally, there is no limitation on the amount of your traditional

49 "Taxpayer Relief Act of 1997 Definition," Investopedia, last updated February 3, 2023, https://www.investopedia.com/terms/t/taxpayer-relief-act-of-1997.asp.
50 "Roth IRAs," Kiplinger, accessed May 1, 2023, https://www.kiplinger.com/retirement/retirement-plans/roth-iras.
51 "The Role of IRAs in US Households' Saving for Retirement, 2020," Investment Company Institute, January 2021, https://www.ici.org/doc-server/pdf%3Aper27-01.pdf.
52 Lorie Konish, "The Biggest Things You Probably Don't Know About Roth IRAs," CNBC, February 20, 2020, https://www.cnbc.com/2020/02/20/the-biggest-things-you-probably-dont-know-about-roth-iras.html.

IRA account balance that you can convert to a Roth IRA in any given year.[53]

I have been speaking of converting traditional IRAs to Roth IRAs, but I want to be sure to note other types of tax-deferred accounts that can also qualify to be converted to Roth IRAs. Almost all retirement plans—including 401(k)s, 403(b)s, 457s, thrift savings plans (TSPs), pension plans, deferred compensation plans, proceeds from employee stock ownership plans (ESOPs), and profit-sharing plans—are candidates to be transferred via trustee-to-trustee transfer (which avoids many IRA rollover limitations—more on that later). They can be transferred directly into an IRA account and then converted into a Roth IRA account.

The Roth Conversion Process

I suggest transferring the retirement funds to an IRA first and then converting it to a Roth IRA using the same IRA custodian you use for the IRA to Roth IRA conversion. The IRA custodian is able to control the correct reporting of the Roth IRA conversion on the 1099-R.

When you transfer an IRA from one custodian to another custodian, before the money is moved, the receiving custodian has to send a letter of acceptance back to the holding custodian. The letter of acceptance verifies that the funds will be maintained inside the conduit of a tax-deferred account.

When you hold a 401(k) through your employer and the money is

---

53 Greg Daugherty, "Roth IRA Conversion Rules," Investopedia, last updated March 23, 2023, https://www.investopedia.com/roth-ira-conversion-rules-4770480.

converted directly to a Roth IRA, it becomes an issue that the custodian reports the 1099-R as the taxable event. You may have to report it as a rollover on your individual tax return, triggering the once-per-year rule. (See "The Once-per-Year Rule" later in this chapter.)

From my experience, it's much easier to use a direct transfer from a 401(k) into a traditional IRA and then convert the IRA account into a Roth IRA account with the same custodian—there's control on both sides of the transaction. And when the 1099-R is reported, there's a much better chance that it's going to be reported using the correct tax code. Making sure that you use a trustee-to-trustee transfer will help keep this transaction as a nontaxable event. Normally this transaction does not have to be reported on your tax return.

Trying to persuade your old company's 401(k) or IRA custodian to issue a corrected 1099-R is difficult at best, and many times it can be nearly impossible to achieve. That leaves you to fight it out with the IRS to try to get it right. That can create a lot of unwanted work and unnecessary anxiety.

Before You Convert to a Roth IRA

Before you convert your traditional IRA to a Roth IRA, you want to look at all your other sources of income for that year. First and foremost, you want to prepare a preliminary tax plan—in essence, a pro forma—that considers your household income, real estate deals, and other taxable events.

By May and June, we have started mapping out our clients' tax plans for the current year.

Using the tax bracket strategy we outlined in chapter 3, you can calculate how much you want to convert to a Roth IRA without triggering too much in additional taxes.

If you don't have a Roth IRA account, you can open one with a zero balance and have it ready to receive your IRA to Roth IRA conversion proceeds.

The Once-per-Year Rule

Once every 365 days, you can make one IRA account rollover.[54] That means you can make only one IRA rollover from any one of your IRA or other retirement accounts to another IRA account. In order for a distribution to qualify specifically as a "rollover," the IRA or 401(k) custodian has to make the check payable to you and mail it to you. Generally, we advise you to avoid IRA rollovers at all costs if possible.

Once you have a new IRA account open, you can determine what your tax bracket will potentially be and how much you want to convert. Then you can look at where you are in the year financially and act accordingly.

I recommend that clients look for dips in the market. Every year on average, the S&P 500 will have a dip of 14.3%.[55] If you own stock within your IRA—for example, let's say Microsoft—the time to con-

---

54 "Rollovers of Retirement Plan and IRA Distributions," IRS, accessed May 1, 2023, https://www.irs.gov/retirement-plans/plan-participant-employee/rollovers-of-retirement-plan-and-ira-distributions.

55 "Annual Returns and Intra-Year Declines," J.P. Morgan, https://am.jpmorgan.com/us/en/asset-management/adv/insights/market-insights/guide-to-the-markets/guide-to-the-markets-slides-us/equities/gtm-annualreturns/.

vert the Microsoft stock in your IRA to your Roth IRA is when the market is down—that's when you want to make the "in-kind" Roth conversion. Because when the market comes back, all that future growth in Microsoft will be inside of your Roth IRA, and all that growth will be income tax–free.

Tackle Your RMD

Another component to your Roth conversion strategy is your age. If you have to take an RMD, you will want to take your RMD distribution early in the year. (Currently, the RMD age is 73 years old, increasing to 75 with the new SECURE Act 2.0.) We recommend that clients take their RMDs in January or February of a given year. But be sure to tackle the RMD before you attempt to affect a Roth conversion. Be sure that the first dollars out of your IRA each year count toward your RMD and are taxable. So, in order to avoid additional taxes, tackle the RMD first, then make your Roth conversion after that.

The money in your Roth IRA is not subject to RMDs.

Paying for Roth IRA Taxes

A whole other wrinkle involves paying for the taxes on the money you convert to your Roth IRA.

A lot of tax and financial professionals will suggest paying for the taxes out of nonqualified money, meaning taxable money that has already been taxed. Think of this as your taxable money that you hold in savings, or a taxable brokerage, or taxable investment account.

Using nonqualified money is the most efficient way to pay for the taxes on the Roth IRA conversion, and it leaves more of your IRA balance available for future Roth IRA conversions.

On the other hand, if you're retired and in your seventies, and you've got a big IRA ($1 million or more), and you're having a hard time being able to convert it before the tax rates increase in 2026, you can pay the taxes on the Roth conversion out of your IRA account.

We make IRA to Roth IRA conversions some time after the RMD has been taken earlier in the year, and then we wait for what we call the "November list." In November, we go through all our clients and identify the clients who want us to pay their income taxes for the year with an IRA distribution. In November, we make a distribution where 100% of the distribution is pushed to federal and state taxes.

The IRS treats those payments as if they were made equally in all four quarters—even though the IRA distribution was not made until November of the tax year. The client is not subject to estimated tax payments, they didn't have to write a check, they didn't have to make any estimated tax payments, and they didn't have to track estimated tax payments. Our clients love this. They did not have to mail a check to the IRS and hope that it arrived in time for the estimated tax payment deadline.

They did pay their estimated taxes due out of their IRA account balance, and they're diminishing the size of that IRA because they're paying taxes with it and making Roth IRA conversions with it.

In my experience, clients *love* paying their taxes out of their IRA accounts. And even though it may not ultimately be the very best financial option, it's a close second. It can be a good solution because it means they're not dipping into their Roth IRAs.

Qualified Charitable Distributions (QCD)

For clients over 70 and a half years old who own IRA accounts, qualified charitable distributions (QCDs) offer a chance to satisfy their RMDs while excluding that amount from taxable income.

If you have a college alma mater, or a church, or another charity you volunteer for, and you have an annual social obligation to make a charitable gift every year, you can make that gift out of your IRA. You deposited the money tax-deferred into your IRA account, and it grew tax-deferred, and then you can give it away and don't have to recognize any taxable income. The charity doesn't have to recognize any taxes either because it is a nonprofit—and you get credit toward your RMD for the year.

The only one who loses out is Uncle Sam. The QCD is one of the best tax moves available.

The Right Time to Use Your Roth IRA Money

While the money in your Roth IRA is your most sacred money, there are sometimes good reasons to use it earlier rather than later.

Pulling some money out of your Roth IRA in a year where you need more income could keep you from making your Social Security taxable or perhaps prevent you from pushing your income into a higher tax bracket. You might reach into various income or investment buckets to make up your annual income, but otherwise, you will generally want to allow your Roth IRA to grow tax-free as long as possible.

With the Roth IRA, once you contribute to it or convert IRA money into your Roth IRA from your traditional IRA, the amount of that conversion is available to you, tax- and penalty-free, assuming you have met the five-year holding period.

The Five-Year Holding Period

A five-year holding period affects the taxability or penalty on the growth inside your Roth IRA account if you have held the account for less than five years. So, if you've been converting to a Roth IRA for three years and you need to take some money out of the account, as long as the amount you remove is less than the amount you con-verted over that time, there is no additional penalty for taking that money out—even if you are under age 59.

You want to get that five-year window open and running on your Roth IRA as soon as possible. You will want to open the account, contribute a little bit of money to get the account working, and get that five-year clock running so that, as long as it's been open for five years and you're over 59 and one-half years old, all future dis-tributions are qualified distributions and are not subject to penal-ties or taxes.

CHAPTER 9

ROTH IRA MYTHS

Over the Years, I Have Run into Many Myths and Erroneous Beliefs About Roth IRAs. Hopefully You Can Avoid Them!

"A Roth 401(k) or a Roth IRA takes the uncertainty out of predicting the future."

—ED SLOTT[56]

Misinformation or an incorrect belief window can cause you to take steps that can be very damaging—or very expensive—and take you off track in your move to tax-free. And the consequences can be devastating.

Let's look at a hypothetical couple named Dick and Barbara. Both are retired and they each own a large IRA account. They are interested in converting their IRAs to Roth IRAs. Dick was worried about all the income taxes that they would have to pay on both IRA

---

56 Gail Marks Jarvis, "Roth 401(k)s May Bring Peace of Mind," *Baltimore Sun*, March 5, 2006, https://www.baltimoresun.com/os-xpm-2006-03-05-roth05-story.html.

accounts. The wrong information was causing him to incorrectly avoid converting any part of his IRA to a Roth IRA. He incorrectly believed that he had to convert his entire IRA account to a Roth IRA, all at one time, in the same tax year. Apparently, he had never heard of using the tax bracket strategy. He was only considering the pain he would experience by converting his entire multimillion-dollar IRA account *all at once* and then having to pay the tax bill.

He did not know that there are other Roth IRA conversion strategies. He did not know about or understand how to use the tax bracket strategy to convert his IRA to a Roth IRA systematically over a number of years, keeping his taxes lower and still providing him with the opportunity to move his entire IRA or 401(k) to a tax-free Roth IRA account.

When he found out that my firm prepares an annual tax plan for our clients, then he wanted to learn how he could use the tax bracket strategy for himself and Barbara. Let me tell you how we implement the tax bracket strategy for our clients. First we calculate the potential tax brackets, and create a tax plan to convert the right amount of IRA to Roth IRA each year specific to their individual situation. This would enable him to convert his IRA to a Roth IRA in just the right amounts each year to keep him in the tax bracket we have planned for together. Over the years, I have run into many myths and erroneous beliefs about Roth IRAs. I would like to enumerate some of the more common myths that can mislead you regarding your Roth IRA and the choices and benefits it can provide for you.

Myth #1: I have to convert my entire traditional IRA account (or accounts) all at once if I make a Roth conversion.

When you don't convert your entire IRA account to a Roth IRA, that is considered a *partial* Roth conversion. Partial Roth conversions have been allowed for many years now. They allow you, with proper tax planning, to convert just the right amount of your IRA to a Roth IRA in order to stay within the tax bracket of your choosing.

Using a partial Roth conversion, you can systematically convert your traditional IRA to a Roth IRA over a number of years without bumping yourself into a marginal tax bracket that is too high.

Myth #2: There are limitations on the amount of my IRA account I can convert to a Roth IRA at one time or in any given tax year.

One of the beauties of the IRA to Roth conversion is that there are no limitations on the amount of IRA that you can convert to a Roth IRA in any given tax year. If Bill Gates wanted to convert his entire IRA or 401(k) to a Roth IRA, he could do it, even if it was $10 million or more. There have been proposals to limit who can make an IRA to Roth conversion based on income. The Biden Build Back Better plan is an example; it would have stopped couples with taxable income greater than $450,000 from being able to make a Roth conversion. It was never passed.

Myth #3: If I am still working, I cannot make a Roth IRA conversion.

If you own a traditional IRA, you can convert it to a Roth IRA at any age. Your employment status has no influence on your ability to make a Roth IRA conversion. That said, you will want to wait until you are over 59 and one-half years old before you draw funds out of your IRA due to the 10% early withdrawal penalty. Prior to age 59 and one-half, make sure that you have the necessary funds available that are required to pay the tax (federal and state) for the IRA to Roth IRA conversion.

Myth #4: I should wait until the end of the year to make my Roth conversion, so my IRA account has had more time to grow.

Let me ask you a question. Which would you choose: to let your money grow in your traditional tax-deferred IRA all year, or to let your money grow inside of your tax-free Roth IRA account? Most people would like to have their money growing tax-free so that the dividends and growth of the account will not be subject to federal income tax in the future.

In most cases, you will likely want to convert to a Roth IRA earlier rather than later in the year, allowing your Roth IRA to capture that growth and save it for your future retirement income tax–free.

Myth #5: My income is too high for me to make a Roth conversion.

There are no income restrictions on making Roth IRA conversions. So, no matter how much you earn, you are free to make a Roth conversion whenever you like.

Myth #6: If I contribute to a Roth IRA, or make a Roth IRA conversion, I will have to wait five years to take a distribution.

It is true that there is a five-year holding period, and you must be 59 and one-half years before you can take out qualified distributions from your Roth IRA account.

However, a taxpayer may always take out the amount that they have contributed to a Roth IRA at any time, tax- and penalty-free. It is only when you seek to pull out the growth prior to the five-year holding period that you may subject the earnings to taxation and penalties.

Roth conversions are not available for tax- and penalty-free distribution until you have held the conversion amount for five years. Each separate conversion has a separate five-year waiting period. Roth conversion dollars are available tax- and penalty-free if distributed after five years or after age 59 and one-half.

Myth #7: I don't trust the government. Even though I have already paid the taxes on my Roth IRA conversion, the government might try to tax it a second time.

What makes you think that the government wants to tax your Roth IRA a second time any more than it wants to just raise the taxes on other money that you have? If the government wanted to stop Roth IRAs and not allow them anymore, I envision a change similar to the divorce deduction law in 2019. Prior to that law taking effect, after a divorce where a husband had been the breadwinner, if he was paying alimony to his ex-wife, he could receive a tax deduction for the alimony he paid, while she had to recognize that income for the alimony, she received as if she had worked for it and earned it. That law took away the tax deduction for paying alimony, and the alimony received no longer had to be recognized as taxable income. When that law was passed, anyone divorced before that point got grandfathered in with the old law. If there is a change with Roth IRAs at some point in the future, I believe those people who currently own Roth IRAs will be grandfathered in. And the rest of you who don't own a Roth IRA when they close the barn doors, well, I am sorry, but it will be too late for you.

Myth #8: I'm better off keeping my money in my traditional IRA account.

When you own a traditional IRA or 401(k), you are leaving it to the government of the future to impose whatever tax rates they wish on you. It's like investing in the stock market. Do you really trust the government not to raise the tax rates on you going into the future over the next 20–30 years?

When you own a Roth IRA, every penny in that account is yours, and there are no future federal or state taxes. They can't increase the taxes, and they can't take a portion of your Roth IRA away from you because you now own the entire account. The way to ensure that what you own for retirement is completely yours, without a potential IRS IOU attached to it, is to convert your traditional tax-deferred accounts (traditional IRAs and 401(k)s) to Roth IRA accounts. Otherwise, you don't have any assurance, only uncertainty, as to what future tax rates will be on your retirement account balances.

If (when) tax rates go higher in the future like they most certainly will have to in order to pay for the national debt, to pay for our underfunded social insurance programs like Social Security and Medicare, and to service the interest on the national debt at new higher interest rates, not to mention inflation—leaving your money in a traditional IRA will almost ensure that you will have to pay higher taxes on it (in the future) than if you would have converted it to a Roth IRA account today while tax rates are on sale compared to historical tax rates in the United States.

CHAPTER 10

THE TOOLS WE USE FOR TAX-FREE INCOME

You Can Mix and Match the Tools—and the Tools You Use Can Vary by Year

"Men have become the tools of their tools."

—HENRY DAVID THOREAU[57]

*L*et's examine the tools you should be considering in your effort to begin moving to tax-free. Some of these tools were already highlighted earlier. The beauty of these strategies is that you can mix and match them—and the tools you use can vary by year.

For many years now the Roth IRA has been the preferred "go-to" tax-free vehicle that we as tax professionals have recommended to clients. In December of 2019, the U.S. government approved the SECURE Act. The biggest change included in the SECURE Act was the termination of the "Stretch IRA" benefit for your children when

---

57 Henry David Thoreau, *Walden* (London: CRW Publishing Limited, 2004), 43.

they inherit your IRA.[58]

Before the SECURE Act, your children were able to "stretch" out the RMDs over their remaining lifetimes. With the SECURE Act, your child will now have to cash in the entire Roth IRA within 10 years of your death.

Wow! Want to talk about a legacy estate planning killer. The SECURE Act changed the Roth IRA from one of the preeminent tax-free legacy wealth transfer tools to just another account that will have to be paid out in full within 10 years of the death of the IRA owner.

The Roth IRA can be very good as a tax-free retirement savings vehicle. But after the SECURE Act, it is no longer the preferred and preeminent wealth transfer tool it used to be.

Just last year, in 2023, it became very evident to me—more so than at any time in the past—that the LIRP has become far more important as a tax-free legacy and wealth transfer tool than ever before. The Roth IRA can no longer fulfill its role as an ideal wealth transfer tool due to the SECURE Act's new 10-year distribution rule for non-EDBs (eligible designated beneficiaries).

This new rule cripples Roth IRAs from being able to help your children continue to grow their inheritance from you in a tax-free environment.

This has made the LIRP a much more important tax-free diversification tool than it was prior to this rule.

When we have historically discussed funding tax-free investment

---

58 "SECURE Act Rewrites the Rules on Stretch IRAs," Fidelity, February 8, 2023, https://www.fidelity.com/learning-center/personal-finance/retirement/secure-act-inherited-iras.

vehicles, we would recommend that tax-deferred funds (qualified funds) from your 401(k) and traditional IRA accounts should primarily be used to fund a Roth IRA conversion account. Since the SECURE Act, that is no longer the clear path you should take to create tax-free investment accounts. It has now become prudent to fund both a Roth conversion IRA and a LIRP.

Creating a diversified and balanced portfolio of tax-free investment vehicles and tax-free income sources is more important now than ever before.

Let's dig into some of the tax-free tools you can use to create tax-free income in your retirement and tax-free income (and tax-free lump sums) you can leave to your heirs.

The Roth IRA Conversion

The Roth IRA conversion involves converting your traditional 401(k) or traditional IRA into a Roth IRA. Assuming that you are 59 and one-half years old and have met the five-year holding period when you begin to take distributions from these accounts, you will not owe any penalties or taxes on those distributions.

The Roth IRA conversion account can be invested in almost any asset class that you choose. It can provide you with great investment flexibility and is available in almost every investment platform imaginable, including brokerage accounts that can hold stocks, bonds, mutual funds, ETFs, and many types of alternative investments including real estate in REITs, separately managed accounts, private equity, and more. You can also invest in and use annuities.

The Roth IRA conversion account is the primary vehicle that many of you will use to convert your tax-deferred savings (traditional IRAs and 401(k) plan proceeds) into Roth IRAs. There is no limit on how much you can convert to a Roth IRA in any given year. A partial IRA to Roth IRA conversion is allowed as well, so you can convert any dollar amount that you desire.

When you convert tax-deferred funds from an IRA or 401(k), for example, you have to recognize the amount you are converting to the Roth IRA or Roth 401(k) as taxable income. The tax rate will be determined by your other taxable income that year, other deductions, and tax credits. This is a big deterrent to some taxpayers and to some other tax professionals who have not yet fully embraced the likelihood of much higher income tax rates in the U.S. in the future.

Leaving your money in tax-deferred accounts (IRA or 401(k)) subjects you to the risk of those potentially higher tax rates in the future. You won't ever really know how much of your IRA account is really yours until you finally draw it out.

The Roth IRA Contribution Account

The Roth IRA contribution account allows account holders to contribute an after-tax permitted amount each tax year, currently around $7,000 per year for account holders under age 50 ($8,000 for those 50 years old and older). As a result, these accounts do not generally grow as large as 401(k) Roth accounts, which may allow as much as $30,500 (in 2024) to be contributed in a single tax year. Like the Roth conversion IRA, these accounts may be invested in almost any asset class and are widely available in almost every retirement plan platform.[59]

The Roth 401(k)

The Roth 401(k) is a newer animal. Roth 401(k) contributions only became available to plan participants in 2006.[60]

Compare that to the traditional 401(k), which was created in 1978.[61] No wonder many people aren't as familiar with the Roth 401(k). If you haven't engaged a financial planner, a proactive tax accountant, or an investment advisor who's helping you create a long-term financial plan, this option probably hasn't been on your radar.

People in your company's HR department only know what they know. Some companies even have automatic enrollment in a retirement plan. And when employees choose a plan for themselves, they're more likely to choose options they are familiar with—which in most cases tends to mean choosing a traditional tax-deferred 401(k).

There's a learning curve required with these strategies, especially when delayed gratification is concerned.

With a traditional 401(k), you're getting the deduction on the front end—you don't have to recognize your 401(k) contribution amounts as taxable income for that year. That's attractive to a lot

---

59 Jean Folger, "Roth IRA vs. 401(k): What's the Difference?," Investopedia, last updated March 31, 2023, https://www.investopedia.com/ask/answers/100314/whats-difference-between-401k-and-roth-ira.asp.

60 John E. Buckley, "Another Retirement Savings Option: Roth 401(k) Plan," U.S. Bureau of Labor Statistics, February 22, 2006, https://www.bls.gov/opub/mlr/cwc/another-retirement-savings-option-roth-401k-plan.pdf.

61 Dom Difurio, "Evolution of the 401(k)," Guideline, September 13, 2022, https://www.guideline.com/blog/evolution-of-401k.

of people because they get to pay less taxes on their wages for the current year.

The downside is that you don't get the long-term benefits of delayed gratification. If that money is shifted to a Roth 401(k), it will never be taxed by the federal or state government again. *Ever.* That's a long time. Why can I say that? Because it's already been taxed. It's highly unlikely that the government will try double taxation as a strategy. It will likely be met with violence and some very motivated voters—not a good situation for politicians.

Additionally, this tax-free account can potentially allow you to accumulate tax-free dollars faster than with traditional IRA accounts, due to the size of the contribution that's allowed each year. Currently (as of 2024), individuals over 50 years of age may contribute $30,500 annually.[62] The Roth 401(k) will only allow you to invest in the investment choices made available inside of your Roth 401(k) plan.

If you are 59 and one-half years old, many company plans will allow you to make an **"in-service distribution"** and make a trustee-to-trustee transfer from your Roth 401(k) into a Roth IRA account.

Making a trustee-to-trustee transfer of this kind is not a taxable event and will allow you to manage the proceeds in any investment vehicle of your choosing inside of a Roth IRA account.

The new Roth IRA account will have an almost unlimited selection of investment possibilities available to you, providing you with

---

62 Jean Folger, "Roth IRA vs. 401(k): What's the Difference?," Investopedia, last updated March 31, 2023, https://www.investopedia.com/ask/answers/100314/whats-difference-between-401k-and-roth-ira.asp.https://www.investopedia.com/ask/answers/100314/whats-difference-between-401k-and-roth-ira.asp.

a much wider selection of investment choices than will be available inside of your Roth 401(k) plan. This can provide you with wider latitude in taking control of your investment performance and risk.

The Life Insurance Retirement Plan (LIRP)

I want to ask you to pause for a moment and ask yourself a few questions:

- Do I have a negative view of life insurance?
- Do I see permanent cash-value life insurance as a positive?

If you have a negative view of permanent cash-value life insurance, I want to invite you to take your negative thoughts and put them on a shelf for a few minutes. Consider that maybe you don't know everything about life insurance.

Ask yourself these questions:

- What do wealthy people know that I don't know? Because the very wealthy have been using life insurance extensively for many years.
- Is it cheaper to rent a house or to buy a house, over the long run?

You see, sometimes you have to put context to what you are considering and look at aspects that perhaps you did not know applied to the situation.

Please keep an open mind. I used to be against life insurance as an investment vehicle. Now that I am looking at it through the lens of the U.S. tax system and all the future fiscal problems our country is facing, as I have laid out in this book, it takes on a whole new meaning and importance.

The life insurance retirement plan (LIRP) is structured differently than you would normally imagine you would structure a permanent life insurance policy.

Historically, when a person purchases a permanent life insurance policy, they are trying to buy the largest amount of death benefit for the least amount of premium. When we are structuring a LIRP, we structure the policy in just the opposite manner—we are trying to purchase the least amount of death benefit required by the IRS for the amount of premium we want to invest into the policy.

We are seeking to invest the largest amount of premium allowed by the IRS relative to the death benefit. The funds invested into a permanent cash-value life insurance policy are allowed to grow income tax–free inside of the policy.

This method of structuring a LIRP allows the instrument to potentially shelter all the growth inside the policy from taxes as it grows, and as you take policy loans or cost-basis distributions from the policy to generate tax-free retirement income. As I explained back in Chapter 5, when an insurance company provides you with a policy loan, they will usually charge you an interest rate on the loan amount. Currently many insurance companies charge around 4% as a policy loan interest rate. This provides you with the opportunity for arbitrage if the investment strategy is positive for the year. Historically, many investment strategies provide performance in the 4% to 7% range over long periods of time.

The index could also provide performance of zero if the investment strategy usually tied to an index like the S&P 500 is negative for the year. If the investment strategy index is negative for that year your performance would be zero; you would not lose principal in the investment account if you are using an indexed universal life policy (IUL).

However, you would be charged the interest amount for the loan, and that would be charged against the cash value in your policy. In such a case, your cash value could drop by the amount of interest on the loan that is charged to the account for that year.

In years where the investment strategy index performs well, then you can add additional growth to the account through the use of loan policy arbitrage. The investment strategy outperforming the policy loan interest rate can provide that extra growth to the cash value of the policy.

Unlike the Roth IRA, you can borrow funds over a number of years, and then when you come into new money to invest (say you inherit funds, or you sell a business, real estate, or some other asset), you can invest a large amount all at once, paying off all of the previous loans. This flexibility makes the LIRP a very powerful tax-free retirement vehicle. In fact this ability to invest additional funds and then take them out again makes this one of the most powerful and potent tax-free investment vehicles.

Then, at the moment it's needed most, the LIRP can provide tax-free death benefits to your loved ones at your death, providing them with a tax-free wealth transfer death benefit.

The evolution of the LIRP in recent decades parallels the evolution of mobile phone technology. First, we had car phones, which were built into our vehicles. Then there were bag phones, which were the size of a brick. Then we got to the age of beepers and flip phones. From there, we had the BlackBerry, with all its buttons, and now smartphones. There's even been dramatic evolution from early smartphones to the smartphones of today, which have more computing power than the mainframes in decades past.

Much the same way, the permanent cash-value life insurance industry has developed and evolved. New instruments such as the IUL, which uses strategies that participate in the performance of indexes, but where your funds are invested in the general account of the insurance company, never at risk from the downdrafts of the equity markets. Variable universal life (VUL) policies can provide you with the growth potential afforded by the ability to invest in—and fully participate in—the stock market indexes, including the S&P 500. These policies also allow you the full up- and downside of the stock market performance. Some people want that. Others want to be more protected, even though they may have to give up some upside potential.

Usually, when you are using the IUL, the investment into one of the investment segments will participate in the growth of the index with a cap, the maximum that you can expect to earn in the market for that year. Let's say the cap is 9%. If the stock market goes up 12%, your earnings will be limited to the cap of 9%. On the other hand, they can also offer downside protection against a drop in the market. So if the stock market drops 15%, the IUL will usually have a floor of zero, so you will not participate in the losses of the index that year.

IUL cash-value insurance policies usually will have an investment segment with an annual point to point with a cap. Currently, many caps are running around 8% to 10% per year.

Those who would like the opportunity for greater potential performance can purchase VUL policies, which can allow allocations to subaccounts, that can provide the potential for full participation in the upside performance of a given market. When considering using variable life insurance policies for supplemental retirement income, it's important to note that underperformance of the policy's subaccounts may require increased premium payments to prevent a policy lapse. In the event of a policy lapse or termination, outstanding loans will be deemed a taxable payment to you as the investor.

Some IUL policies offer performance factors (for an additional cost) to leverage and multiply the performance of the investment index (i.e., S&P 500), providing the opportunity to achieve additional growth performance. For example, one company provides a performance factor that will multiply the investment strategy performance by 2.7 times.

These new developments have become major game changers in how life insurance is able to perform as an investment class. The LIRP vehicle can provide potential lifetime tax-free income after an appropriate waiting period—usually 5 to 10 years.

Recent developments also allow the LIRP to potentially provide accelerated death benefits to the policy owner, which can provide for long-term care benefits. These benefits generally come with no additional cost as an added perk to the policy.

The LIRP is not available to everyone. You or one of your loved ones must meet certain health requirements to qualify for this policy.

If you try to overfund your life insurance policy too quickly, the IRS has rules where they will make your life insurance policy change to a modified endowment contract, or "MEC," which loses the major benefits that permanent cash value life insurance can provide. In simple terms, a MEC takes away your ability to provide tax-free loan proceeds as a future source of retirement income. It changes the life insurance policy so it can only provide tax-deferred growth very similar to a tax-deferred annuity. This puts you right back in the position of having tax-deferred growth, only to have to pay ordinary income tax at higher tax rates in the future.

Instead of creating tax-free income in retirement, you will now only have tax-deferred growth, and all that growth will be taxed in the future, at potentially much higher tax rates and as ordinary income. And if the tax rates go higher as we all fear, you have completely blown the potential tax-free benefits that would have been yours inside of your permanent cash value life insurance policy.

Unlike the Roth IRA, which has limitations on how much you can contribute to that account, the LIRP has no such limitations, meaning LIRP owners can contribute large amounts to these accounts, providing for a larger and healthier tax-free retirement income stream. The other huge benefit to a LIRP is that you can borrow funds from the policy (income tax–free) and then, at a later date, replace the funds back into the policy, allowing them to continue to grow income tax–free. Being able to flexibly borrow money from your LIRP policy and then pay it back later can provide you with some very interesting planning options. Certainly, once you pull funds from your Roth IRA, you cannot contribute them back into the Roth IRA account at a later date. This is a huge benefit that the LIRP can provide to you and your family.

Arbitrage is also a large benefit that the LIRP can provide to the policy owner. When you borrow funds, the insurance company leaves your money invested and will loan you funds from the general account of the insurance company. They will charge you an interest rate; for now, that rate is around 4%. Usually these accounts are expected to earn 5% to 7%.

Consider the impact of this example. As you borrow funds for income from your LIRP, the funds are left invested, earning 5% to 7%. You are borrowing funds at 4%. The difference of 2% to 3% that you get to earn on your account balance is arbitrage. It continues to provide additional growth to your policy over the years as you take retirement income. This benefit of receiving arbitrage earnings on your withdrawals is not available to a Roth IRA or any other investment vehicle that I can think of.

I am convinced now more than at any time in the past that a LIRP is a very important asset class that almost every family should consider owning. I am not alone in that conclusion. Ernst & Young, in their October 2022 research titled "Benefits of Integrating Insurance Products into a Retirement Plan," have found that most people would benefit from placing 30% to 50% of their retirement assets into a permanent cash-value life insurance policy.[63]

With the Roth IRA having its ability to stretch tax-free benefits

---

63 "Benefits of Integrating Insurance Products into a Retirement Plan," Ernst & Young, accessed May 1, 2022, https://assets.ey.com/content/dam/ey-sites/ey-com/en_us/topics/insurance/ey-benefits-of-integrating-insurance-products-into-retirement-plan.pdf?download.

now limited to just 10 years due to the SECURE Act, the LIRP has now moved into the number one position for creating tax-free income strategies for both you and your beneficiaries.

The Reverse Mortgage and the Reverse Mortgage Line of Credit

First, let me address the elephant in the room. Many people harbor negative thoughts and feelings toward reverse mortgages. They have heard bad things. They are not familiar with reverse mortgages, and most of us are fearful of and naturally avoid things that we don't understand or that we don't have any experience with.

Most of us have used and are familiar with a regular 30-year forward-looking home mortgage. We are used to them and are comfortable using them. We know what to expect. These newfangled reverse mortgages can't be any good, can they? We have never used one before, and we don't know a lot about them, and certainly we are not about to bet the farm (or our house) on one, just in case something about it goes bad.

I understand. I know that I am talking to you about a mortgage vehicle that you may not have heard a lot about, nor have you had time to learn about them, or even had an interest in doing so. I can see how that might be scary.

But in fact, a reverse mortgage can be a flexible and very useful financial planning instrument to provide tax-free access to the equity in your home. A reverse mortgage or a reverse mortgage line of credit can generate tax-free funds that can be used as tax-free income in retirement.

First, let me make it clear. I don't sell reverse mortgages. I do not receive any direct remuneration if you decide to use one or not.

I don't have a dog in this fight, other than I want my clients to consider all their financial planning options with an open mind, looking objectively at the choices before them. I want the same for you, my reader.

I do, however, know a lot about reverse mortgages and the strategies you can use to then provide your family with their tax-free benefits.

Let's identify the various ways you can use a reverse mortgage or a reverse mortgage line of credit as a financial-planning and tax-planning tool. We will identify some of the requirements to qualify for one of the reverse mortgage loans, and then who may benefit from using them, and who may not. Finally, I will provide you with the considerations, costs, risks, and potential negatives of these instruments.

If after all of that you find the reverse mortgage or the reverse mortgage line of credit interesting, then I would encourage you to speak with your financial advisor about ways in which you can use a reverse mortgage or a reverse mortgage line of credit to obtain tax-free income in retirement. Here are the strategies you might consider using to employ a reverse mortgage or a reverse mortgage line of credit.

Stop Making a Mortgage Payment in Retirement

This would be what I would consider to be the first foundational use of a reverse mortgage.

If you are retired, over the age of 62, and are still making a house payment in retirement, one of the reverse mortgage strategies is that it could help you lower your cash flow requirements in retirement. Here are some of the key questions that can help you evaluate if this strategy may be one that fits your situation.

- Is this your last house? (That means you don't expect to buy another house.)
- Do you expect one of your children will want to move into your house after you die? Or will they just sell it?
- Are you OK with your children selling the house after you die and pocketing the money from the proceeds?
- If you did not have to make your current house payment, what would you like to do with the extra tax-free cash flow that is freed up?

Many people in retirement are drawing money out of their IRA account and paying taxes on it in order to just make a house payment.

Imagine, you are increasing your taxable income, potentially making your Social Security taxable, potentially hitting a Medicare IRMAA penalty threshold, in order to make your house payment. You're taking liquid investments and turning them into illiquid equity in your house.

You did not plan on doing it that way. It's just the way life turned out.

By replacing your traditional mortgage with a reverse mortgage, you can stop making house payments (principal and interest). Of course, you will still have to pay property taxes, maintain homeowners insurance, and keep up the maintenance on the home. But the payment on the bank loan will no longer have to be paid every month.

This strategy can help you conserve your liquid resources, providing you with more flexibility in the future for retirement income needs.

When we are creating estate planning options with clients, I'll ask them, "What do you want to have happen to your house when you die?"

"We want to leave the house to the kids," they say.

"Are the kids going to physically move into the house and live there?" I ask.

"No, we're just going to leave them the house."

"So, your kids are going to sell the house after you die and pocket the proceeds?"

"Yes."

"So, if your kids had the choice of receiving the house, or a big pile of tax-free money, which do you think they would prefer to receive?"

In this scenario, many times it's going to be the pile of money. People can do everything I have illustrated above without leaving their house, without selling their home, and without moving.

It's important to consciously recognize and intentionally understand where you are building equity and value. Instead of making a $2,000 mortgage payment each month, you could wind up with an additional $24,000 of tax-free spendable money each year because you are not spending it on a $2,000 monthly mortgage payment.

Let me be clear right here. I am not saying you will take $2,000 of income out of your home in the form of a reverse mortgage. I am saying if you currently have a mortgage payment of $2,000 per month that is made up of principal and interest, the reverse mortgage may relieve you of having to make that payment.

The income that is then freed up from having to be spent on a mortgage payment for principal and interest can then be directed for another purpose, to be spent on other expenses or financial needs, like travel, or gifting, or other goals that you may have.

To be sure, this does not relieve you from the costs still associated with ownership of your home for maintenance and repairs, property taxes, and homeowners insurance. But it can relieve you of the monthly principal and interest payment to the bank for the loan itself.

Reverse mortgages are not for everyone, and further down in this section I will fully address the challenges associated with these strategies.

Use a Reverse Mortgage Line of Credit to Control Your Mortgage Interest Deduction

Currently many retirees are unable to benefit from deducting their mortgage interest because the standard is so high due to the Tax Cuts and Jobs Act in 2017. Many professionals believe that we may maintain the high standard deductions that we have now longer than the sunset provisions at the end of 2025.

By using a reverse mortgage line of credit, you can let mortgage interest accrue over a number of years, and then bunch the mortgage interest tax deduction together with other itemized deductions on your 1040 Schedule A by paying all of the accrued interest at one time in the same tax year.

Your mortgage interest for multiple years will accrue to such an amount that it will potentially become a significant tax deduction because, combined with your other itemized deductions, the amount will likely be more than the standard deduction. The amount of deductible mortgage interest is limited to your acquisition indebtedness, which really means that you can only write off the interest equal to the cost of the home and/or improvements to the home that are financed by the loan.

You can also use the big mortgage interest deduction to offset the taxable income generated by a Roth conversion, allowing you to potentially convert more of your IRA to a Roth IRA.

The Reverse Mortgage Line of Credit Volatility Protection Strategy

The number one risk that we all face in retirement is "**sequence of return risk.**"

If any market (stock, bond, real estate, commodities, crypto, etc.) loses a lot of value early in your retirement, and you're drawing money out of that account at the same time the markets are dropping, your investment portfolio may never be able to recover from the drop in the market and downdraft of your withdrawals. This can potentially cause you to run out of money prematurely. That is "sequence of return risk."

To protect against such a scenario, a reverse mortgage line of credit may be an instrument you can use to provide cash flow flexibility, to assist you in your moment of need when one of the markets drops in value.

Instead of drawing income from your investments invested in one of the markets (stock, bond, real estate, commodities, crypto) that have dropped in value, you can draw down on your reverse mortgage line of credit. The funds you draw from the reverse mortgage line of credit are loan proceeds, and thereby are not taxable income. In fact, they are income tax–free. Because they are tax-free you may not have to draw as much out, because you will not have to cover for income tax.

These loan proceeds can help keep your Social Security from being taxable, and they can also provide the buffer you need to allow the market, whatever it may be, to recover before you need to withdraw income from those investments.

When and if the various markets recover, you can sell the positions in your stock and bond market portfolio and can pay back the reverse mortgage line of credit, paying down the interest that has accumulated over the years (not the interest on the funds you withdrew for living expenses) and potentially creating a large, itemized deduction on your tax return. This strategy can provide tremendous flexibility to your overall tax-free financial plan.

The Reverse Mortgage Line of Credit for Access to Home Equity without Selling or Making House Payments

Traditionally, as Americans we have used the equity in our homes as a piggy bank that we have systematically raided from time to time. Historically, the tool we have used to do that is the home equity line of credit, or HELOC. Usually, these loans are set up with a variable interest only payment. As real estate has gained value, homeowners have borrowed for all kinds of reasons: home improvements, vacations, education, vehicles, and everything else under the sun.

If the proceeds of a HELOC are not used to improve the home, the interest is not tax deductible.

Enter the American baby boomer who is now 62 years old, and a whole new option becomes available: the reverse mortgage line of credit. The reverse mortgage line of credit is different from the traditional HELOC because the borrower is not required to make any monthly payments. The interest is just allowed to accrue on the balance of the loan.

Most reverse mortgage lines of credit employ a variable interest rate similar to the HELOC. One big distinction is that the reverse mortgage line of credit requires about 50% to 60% equity in the home in order to be set up, whereas the HELOC can be set up with as little as 20% to 30% equity depending on the real estate markets and the banking loan requirements at the time.

Why would someone want to use a reverse mortgage line of credit?

The answer is: access to a portion of the equity in your home, using a loan that will not require a monthly payment. This can provide you with access to tax-free funds on demand, giving you the ability to know you have access to additional emergency funds should the need arise. Certainly, the concern that many retirees have is the risk of long-term care expenses, for one or both spouses. The reverse mortgage line of credit can help provide a backup resource should the time come that you are seeking sources of funding for long-term care needs.

Requirements to Qualify for a Reverse Mortgage or a Reverse Mortgage Line of Credit

Here are the major requirements for you to be able to qualify for a reverse mortgage loan, or line of credit. While there are now some competitive non–home equity conversion mortgage (HECM) reverse mortgage loan products on the market, I am primarily teaching you about the government-backed HECM loan requirements. Here is a list of requirements you will want to be aware of before you apply for a reverse mortgage product.

1. **Age.** You must be a homeowner aged 62 or older. If the home is owned by both spouses, you will both need to be age 62+ in order to qualify. There is no upper age limit.

2. **Ownership or primary residence.** You must be the owner of your primary residence. "Primary residence" means just that—just like for tax purposes.

3. **Equity position.** You must either own your home outright, have a low mortgage balance (50% or less), or be able to pay

down your mortgage balance.

4. **No federal debt.** You cannot owe any federal debt, such as federal taxes or federal student loans.

5. **Good shape.** Your home must be in good enough condition that it does not require major renovations to bring it up to property standards. The lender will tell you what repairs you need before you can get a reverse mortgage.

6. **Counseling.** You must receive counseling from a HUD approved reverse mortgage counseling agency. You will have to pay the fee.

I would like you to be aware of some other situations that likely will not qualify for a reverse mortgage.

- Vacation homes and secondary homes do not qualify. Remember, it has to be your primary residence.
- Homes on income-producing land such as a farm are not eligible.
- The reverse mortgage must be the primary lien on your home to qualify.
- If you have a manufactured home, it must have been built after June 15, 1979, you must have the seal present to prove it was built with the federal manufactured home construction and safety standards. It must also sit on a permanent foundation.
- If you have very limited resources (i.e., not sufficient to maintain the home), then you may not qualify.
- It is possible to take out a reverse mortgage with a spouse younger than 62 and list them on the HECM as an eligible nonborrowing spouse. Just because you can do something

does not mean it is a good idea. I am generally not a fan of this idea.

Costs, Risks, and Considerations for Reverse Mortgage Loans and Lines of Credit

Let's address the costs first.

- Reverse mortgage loans and credit lines have loan origination fees similar to regular forward mortgage loans (which cannot exceed $6,000 and are paid to the lender).
- Real estate closing costs similar to a regular 30-year mortgage (appraisal, title, surveys, inspections, recording fees, mortgage taxes, credit checks and other fees).
- Interest and servicing fees.
- Annual mortgage insurance premium, which is .05% of the outstanding mortgage balance.
- Homeowner's insurance and property taxes, which you must keep current.

The front-end cost that can dissuade some homeowners from taking out a reverse mortgage loan or line of credit is the upfront mortgage insurance premium. It will be 2% of the lesser of the home value or the maximum lending limit. You don't normally pay for this out of pocket, it is added to the loan balance. But this is the one primary cost that makes the initial setup costs for a reverse mortgage more expensive than a traditional 30-year mortgage.

Risks

Let's consider some of the risks of a reverse mortgage.

- If you are trying to leave equity in your home as a legacy gift to your heirs, a reverse mortgage will consume a portion of your equity, and there is a risk that in a bad real estate market you may not be able to leave any equity in the house to your heirs. Certainly, you will likely leave less equity. At the same time, if you do not have to make a house payment, you may be able to leave more funds in savings to your heirs.

- If you borrow all the available equity out of your home with a reverse mortgage, you will still need to pay the property taxes and insurance, and you will need to have enough funds to maintain your home. It would usually only be if you are not able to meet the loan requirements that you would risk losing your home.

- Remember, this home has to be your primary residence. You cannot live away at some other address without running afoul of the loan requirements.

- A reverse mortgage does not affect your Social Security benefits.

- A reverse mortgage could affect your ability to qualify for other need-based government programs such as Medicaid or Supplemental Security Income (SSI). If you think you may need one of these programs in the future, it is a good idea to discuss this with a benefits specialist to make sure your eligibility will not be compromised.

- Proceeds of a reverse mortgage loan or line of credit can never be used for investment purposes.

- When you bunch mortgage interest with a reverse mortgage, and pay the mortgage interest back, only the mortgage interest and origination fee are generally deductible. Some of the other fees that have been added to the loan (i.e., nondeductible closing costs) that are not tax deductible will also likely have to be paid at the same time in order to secure the bunched-up mortgage interest deduction.

Considerations

- Many people assume that the reverse mortgage is a loan of last resort. I would submit to you that it can be a strong and flexible financial tool for many retirees.

- If you just can't stomach the thought of a reverse mortgage because it has too many negative connotations for you, that's OK. They are not for everyone.

- There are financial reasons not to use one. I am old enough to use one, but I don't want to give up my 2.5% mortgage interest rate on my 15-year mortgage. I can afford the payments. It makes a lot of sense to keep my current mortgage at such a low interest rate.

- I have seen multimillionaires use a reverse mortgage with great success. You are not too wealthy to use a reverse mortgage for many reasons.

- I have seen people who could have benefited greatly from a reverse mortgage look into it, only to be talked out of it by their greedy children. Be aware of conflicts of interest.

- If you die with a reverse mortgage, your children do not have to pay the loan off immediately. They will have to list the house for sale and will usually get six months to sell it and pay off the loan. They may also be given two optional three-month extensions if requested timely.

Section 121 (Sell Your Primary Residence and Avoid Capital Gains Tax—MFJ)

Section 121 is the section of the tax code that deals with capital gains taxes when you sell your primary residence.

If you are astute and use a section 121 exclusion to your benefit when you sell your house, you can avoid paying capital gains tax on as much as $500,000 in capital appreciation (for married couples filing jointly) or up to $250,000 (for single filers).

The section 121 exclusion can be a powerful tax-free strategy when you get to the point where you're ready to sell your primary home and either downsize and move to a different home or transition to independent or assisted living. Some people actually buy and flip or buy and fix up homes and sell them every two years.

You can use the exclusion only if you owned and used your home as your principal residence for at least two of the five years preceding the sale—the two years do not have to be consecutive. You can use the exclusion no more frequently than once every two years. A partial exclusion may be available, even if you don't meet the two out of five years test, if the primary reason for selling your home is a change in place of employment, for health reasons, or certain other unforeseen circumstances such as death, divorce, and disasters.

For my part, I don't want to move that often! But I personally relied on this strategy when my wife and I sold our home.

In 2021, with all the kids out of the house, we had a house that was just too big for our needs (5,000 square feet). We had made a number of improvements over the years, so we had increased our cost basis with those improvements. If you remember what happened in the housing market in 2021 and into 2022—it was going crazy. We were able to sell and use the entire $500,000 of section 121 to shelter capital gains that we would have had in the house. We were able to avoid paying any capital gains taxes at all.

Think about it: no federal tax, no state tax, and no provisional income. This is a great tax-free tool that you can use to shelter your real estate profits on your primary residence when you sell.

This technique is especially valuable with the spike in real estate values in recent years.

Considerations of the Section 121 Exclusion

- This exclusion is only available for your primary residence. Vacation homes, second homes, and rental properties do not qualify.
- Cost basis rules require you to keep good records on acquisition costs and your costs for improvements you have made to the home. In audit you may have to produce those records.
- I recommend that you keep and maintain a file on all the improvements on your home. When the time comes to sell, you

will have your file with all the additional improvement costs.

Tax-Free Social Security Benefits (When Possible)

Imagine that I have been working with Ron and Cathy, a hypothetical couple, for a number of years. We have been systematically creating a tax plan each year and then converting some of Ron's big IRA account to his Roth IRA account. We are now close to having all of his IRA converted over to a Roth IRA and anticipate being finished in two years. Up until this point, the RMD that Ron has been having to take each year has been making both of their Social Security benefits taxable. Eighty-five percent of their Social Security benefits have been subject to income tax. Once we get the remaining last two years of Roth conversions completed, any future distributions that Ron may take from his Roth IRA account will not be included in their taxable income.

The Social Security benefits that he and Cathy receive will no longer be included in their taxable income because they will not have any other taxable income at that point. Remember, all Roth IRA distributions are not taxable income. Ron and Cathy will begin to enjoy tax-free Social Security benefits for the rest of their lives. It's a beautiful thing.

If you're married filing jointly and your provisional income is over $32,000 a year, then your Social Security benefits may have up to 50% included in taxable income.

For the same couple, if your provisional income rises above $44,000, then your Social Security benefits may be included in taxable income up to 85%. These amounts have not been indexed for inflation. So, for many people, it may not be possible to keep their provisional income below the limits.

If you're receiving $40,000 each year in Social Security benefits as a married couple and are receiving another $40,000 of tax-free Roth IRA distributions on top of that, you could potentially keep your Social Security benefits 100% income tax–free. Imagine, $40,000 Social Security benefits income tax–free. If, on the other hand, you received another $24,000 of taxable income, it could bump your provisional income so that your Social Security benefits would have to be included in your taxable income at 85%. That would be an additional $34,000 of taxable income added to your other taxable income in retirement.

Our goal would be to make all your other income tax-free, thereby not triggering the provisional income limitation and potentially keeping your Social Security benefits 100% income tax–free.

Such a goal requires a dedicated and consistent strategy in repositioning your taxable investments and tax-deferred investments to tax-free investments and strategies.

The 1031 Exchange (Like-Kind Exchange)

The 1031 exchange refers to the section of the tax code that relates to like-kind exchanges of real estate. A 1031 exchange involves exchanging one highly appreciated piece of real estate asset for another piece of real estate. One of the items that is most important to most 1031 exchanges is the amount of income that the new asset will be providing.

Although the income may be partially taxable, the goal of the 1031 exchange is to delay paying the capital gains tax on the highly appreciated asset as well as avoiding recapturing all the depreciation you have claimed over the years. Depreciation recapture on the sale of investment real estate is taxed as ordinary income with a maximum tax rate of 25%. Assuming that you can hold on to the asset long enough, upon your death your heirs may receive a step-up in basis.

A 1031 exchange could offer the possibility of avoiding the capital gains tax and the recapture of depreciation altogether if you die owning a piece of highly appreciated real estate. Your heirs may receive a full step-up in basis to the fair market value as of your date of death.

Many families have used these tax laws to legally avoid capital gains tax on real estate that has been held in the family for decades, much of which has depreciation that has been claimed to the point that the cost basis in the property is almost zero, or certainly very low.

That's how the tax laws are currently written.

In 2021 President Joe Biden took aim at 1031 exchanges in his proposed 2023 budget, proposing a $500,000 cap for each taxpayer ($1 million for married couples filing jointly) on deferrals of gains for like-kind exchanges.[64] The final version of President Biden's tax plan did not include this provision, but the consideration raises grave concerns that at some point in the future we may no longer be able to receive a step-up in basis at the passing of a loved one. Such a

---

64 Edward Fernandez, "Op-Ed: What Biden's Proposed Limits to 1031 Exchanges Mean for Investors and the Economy," CNBC, April 26, 2022, https://www.cnbc.com/2022/04/26/what-bidens-proposed-1031-exchange-limits-mean-for-investors-economy.html.

change in the tax laws would create a tremendous increase in taxes as highly appreciated real estate is handed down from one generation to the next.

The problems with owning real estate can be many. Let's start with the 4 Ts:

1. Taxes: Property taxes to be sure.

2. Tenants: Everyone knows how problematic tenants can be.

3. Toilets: Repair requirements can drive any landlord crazy.

4. Trash: Maintenance of rental real estate can be expensive and painful.

I have found many dedicated real estate investors lose their love of rental real estate after they retire. Many of them feel trapped. They would love to sell their fully depreciated, highly appreciated rental, investment, or business real estate, but they don't want to pay all the capital gains taxes. Nor do they want to recapture all that depreciation and pay the potential maximum tax at 25%.

One of the other reasons many of them are hesitant to try and make a 1031 exchange is that there are many variables that can blow up their 1031 exchange, and then the entire sale can become a taxable event—a circumstance that is fraught with more risk than they care to take on.

Let's examine some of the 1031 exchange requirements.

1. You must purchase another "like-kind" investment property. That means real estate for real estate. You can't exchange a property for a semi-truck or a boat even if it is used for busi-

ness. Real estate for real estate.

2. The replacement property must be of equal or greater value. That means you may have to bring more cash to the transaction or add debt. A purchase for any amount less than the sales price represents "boot." That means taxable income.

3. You must invest all the proceeds of the sales. If you keep any excess funds that is "boot," and you will have to pay capital gains tax on it.

4. The title holder and taxpayer must remain the same. If you put it in an LLC, the LLC is making the exchange and must become the new owner of the new properties. You cannot switch ownership (Individual vs. Partnership) in the middle of the transaction.

5. Honor the time limits. You must identify the new replacement property(s) within 45 days of the sale and then conclude the exchange within 180 days. There are three rules that can be applied to define the identification of the properties.

6. You can't touch the money. You will need to use a qualified intermediary to receive the funds from the sale and then provide them for your new real estate purchase.

7. You can only exchange investment property or property held for business purposes. So no, you cannot exchange your principal residence. A vacation home or a second home won't qualify unless it is rented out.

This is a basic list of what is required in order to use a 1031 exchange. As you can see, it could be pretty easy to blow a 1031 exchange. Now consider the recent and current real estate market where there is a shortage of available real estate for sale. Can you imagine trying to frantically find a property to buy?

Enter Commercial REITs into the 1031 Exchange Markets with the DST—The Delaware Statutory Trust

A REIT stands for a Real Estate Investment Trust. The commercially available REITs allow investors to buy into a diversified portfolio of mostly Class A and Class B commercial properties in all types of commercial real estate from retail, to industrial, office, multifamily hotels, and storage units, to data centers, to distribution warehouses. Most of this is spread all over the country to diversify the portfolio and the risk.

Some nontraded REIT companies have now created 1031 exchange programs that will allow accredited investors to exchange into their DST 1031 programs.

(An accredited investor has to have a net worth [excluding the primary residence] in excess of $1 million, or income in excess of $200,000 individually or $300,000 for couples for the last two years, or professional criteria—investment professionals in good standing, directors and executive officers that sell securities, family clients of family offices that are accredited, and knowledgeable employees for investments in a private fund.)

The DST 1031 programs offer some distinct advantages that can make them attractive to some accredited real estate investors, especially those who are in retirement or close to it and ready to be done as real estate investors but would still like to receive the income from a real estate investment without having to pay the capital gains tax. They still want to receive the income in the form of "mailbox money," but they don't want to hassle with or manage the rental real estate anymore.

The other attractive benefit that the DST 1031 programs offer is that after three years they may allow owners to exchange their direct ownership in real estate for shares of the publicly registered nontraded REIT. This can be effected after three years' ownership of the DST. It is made possible with a 721 exchange, another form of tax-free exchange where the real estate owner trades their real estate ownership in the DST for shares of the nontraded REIT.

This can allow the real estate investor the potential ability to sell off as many or as few of the shares as they desire, on a timetable that is of their choosing subject to the limitations of the program, usually quarterly. But consider the power of this offering. If they make a regular 1031 exchange, it is an all or nothing proposition if the owner needs or wants some liquidity. They have to always trade up to a larger property, or they could make the whole transaction taxable due to the 95% rule. REITs usually have some limitations on share redemptions, and the programs could be suspended in an extreme real estate market. But in most normal real estate markets, they can provide a flexible liquidity option that would not be available to an owner of a regular 1031 exchange property.

The 95% Rule in 1031 Exchanges

"If the purchase of one of the properties fell through, the entire 1031 exchange will be disqualified because the exchanger did not acquire 95%

of the fair market value identified."

You see the problem. The 1031 rules do not allow you to make a partial sale of a traditional 1031 exchange and still avoid recognizing the capital gains due to the 95% rule. The DST strategies may provide a way for the investors to make partial sales (liquidity event) after just three years. Yes, most likely the full amount will be subject to recognition of capital gains tax, but you were not required to sell the entire position to access some of the value and create some extra access to cash.

If the real estate investor is interested in trying to leave the greater portion of the real estate to family at their passing in order to take advantage of the step-up in basis rules, the DST strategies can provide flexibility to the family.

Considerations of the DST 1031 Exchange Program

- Not everyone can qualify for a DST 1031 exchange. First you must be an accredited investor. Second, most of the programs require a real estate transaction size of at least $500,000 or more.

- Properties that still have debt can be problematic for any 1031 exchange. If you pay off the old note, there has to be new debt on the exchange. Some programs are not set up to provide that.

- DST programs have costs associated with them, both upfront and ongoing. As a buyer, you pay the transaction costs when you buy in, similar to a regular real estate sale, except you are paying it on the front end to buy in. On the back end, when you sell shares of the REIT, generally there are not any sales charges or real estate commissions to be paid. However, some programs may have a 1% redemption fee.

- DST programs come and go. Some offerings are better than others (i.e., multifamily verses industrial warehouse). There is a chance that when you are ready to sell, the program you wanted is sold out.

- Usually, the DST programs will reserve a space for you if you know you have a transaction coming up. This is attractive to sellers who want to make sure they can get their 1031 exchange completed. The programs provide more consistent availability of properties to buy than just going out into the real estate market and looking for a rental property that you would want to own, manage, repair, maintain, and deal with required improvements. Since the REIT is handling all of that, they can generally provide a more reliable opportunity to allow you to complete your 1031 exchange with success. Professionally managed, and with mailbox money for income.

- Most DST programs generate a 1099 for tax reporting during the first three years. When your property is absorbed back into the nontraded REIT and you receive units of the operating partnership, it will generally generate a K-1 form.

- You will have to hire and use a qualified intermediary to hold your funds until you are ready to deploy them to buy your DST or your new properties.

- A DST program can be a great backup program if you want to sell but are not sure you can find properties to buy. The DST can allow you to protect your 1031, although nothing is guaranteed, and even the DST option could fail to close timely if you do not give them enough time.

- Advisors who represent and sell DST offerings are paid a commission.

- You will need to have your tax professionals report the 1031 exchange on the tax return of the entity that owns the property being exchanged. It would be very beneficial to have them create a tax plan with the 1031 exchange as a proforma so you can see what to expect for that year.

- The 1031 exchange is reported in the tax year in which the sale of your property took place, not the year it was completed.

- Shares of your DST that are exchanged in a 721 exchange for units in a nontraded REITs operating partnership maintain their character and, if held till death, might also provide a full step-up in basis and tax-free proceeds to your heirs.

- If you live in a community property state and hold the DST/REIT Operating Partnership unit in community property with rights of survivorship (i.e., in your revocable living trust), the surviving spouse can receive a full step-up in basis at the death of the first spouse to die.

- 1031 rules are complex and not easy to comply with. It would be wise to seek experienced professionals to advise you and assist you with one of these transactions.

The Exclusion Ratio on Nonqualified Income Annuities

Nonqualified annuities are annuities where the money is not invested in an IRA account. These annuities have also been called "tax-deferred annuities." These annuities allow the invested principal to grow tax-deferred, similar to an IRA.

Although the principal amount that is originally invested in the annuity is not taxable upon withdrawal, the growth would be taxable, and it will be taxed at ordinary income rates.

The exclusion ratio of a tax-deferred annuity allows an annuity to pay out both the principal untaxed and the growth portion taxed, as an income stream to the beneficiary or the account owner. The benefit of using the exclusion ratio is that, generally, the principal is much bigger than the amount that is grown, so the majority of the payment would be a return of principal and would not be includable in taxable income, thereby providing an opportunity to create an income stream where much of it is not includable in taxable income.

Thus, the exclusion ratio can provide a portion of the payment that would be income tax–free for both federal and state tax purposes. Generally, dealing with these annuities is not a do-it-yourself activity.

Involving an insurance professional who is knowledgeable about the options that are available can provide tremendous benefit. I have found a lot of people who own nonqualified annuities are unaware of many of the benefits that could be available to them if they had an insurance and tax professional who was knowledgeable and competent in this area of tax planning.

LTC (Long-Term Care) Tax-Qualified Benefits

Long-term care can be very expensive. And the longer we live, the more likely it is that we will at some point need long-term care ourselves. For a couple turning 65 today, there's nearly a 70% chance that one of them will need some sort of long-term care.[65]

Betting against that risk is dangerous. Doing so could erode your life's savings, leaving your healthy spouse in a very precarious situation where they have spent all your retirement funds for your long-term care needs, with little left for their own retirement needs. If you have legacy wishes that you wish to leave to your heirs, those wishes can also be put in jeopardy with a long-term care event for you or your spouse. **Asset-based** long-term care involves making a single payment or perhaps paying over a 10- to 20-year period of time. In either case, the premium amounts can never be raised by the insurance company, and the benefits can never be decreased by the insurance company.

These types of policies are set up to become paid-up policies. So after the single premium is paid, or after the period of payments is paid in full, no more premium payments will be due, and the policy will be paid in full. Many of the policies allow you to have a return of premium rider (80%) if you want the option to get your premium paid back. What other types of insurance allow you to get your premiums back? These policies provide a death benefit that is usually greater than the amount of premium you have paid in. The death

---

65 "How Much Care Will You Need?," LongTermCare.gov, last modified February 18, 2020, https://acl.gov/ltc/basic-needs/how-much-care-will-you-need.

benefit is income tax–free to your heirs.

These policies provide a large long-term care pool that will provide for your long-term care needs. One key is that you want to make sure the policy is a tax-qualified policy. If it is, then the benefits of the long-term care policy are not includable in taxable income. In fact, they're income tax–free if used for qualified long-term care expenses.

These policies can provide a tremendous resource to a family right in one of their greatest moments of need, by providing tax-free income when it is needed most. The benefits avoid making Social Security benefits taxable while keeping the rest of the income for that year as close to tax-free as possible.

Securities-Based Lines of Credit: The Non-Purpose Loan

Stan and Joan are successful technology workers. They have a technology-heavy stock portfolio with millions of dollars in it. That is the good news. The bad news is that they have a lot of capital gains in the portfolio. They already pay a very high tax rate due to the good earnings from their tech jobs.

Arizona summers in the Phoenix metro area are very hot. People say, "Oh, it's a dry heat." My answer to them is yes, it is, and so is an oven. Both are too dang hot.

Stan and Joan want to build a house in the Durango, Colorado, area, where it is much more comfortable in the summer. Since they both have tech jobs, they can work remotely and enjoy their summers in Colorado as a family. The problem is that they can't get access to their stock portfolio's value without triggering a big taxable event. Enter the SBLOC, a securities-based line of credit.

A non-purpose loan, also known as a securities-based line of credit (SBLOC), uses the assets in a taxable brokerage account as collateral and can provide tax-free loan proceeds to the owners.

These accounts, although they are similar to a margin loan, enable the owner to borrow more, allowing you to keep the debt separate from the collateral. Generally, these lines of credit also offer lower interest rates than what is generally available on a margin account.

SBLOC accounts can provide you with access to funds when needed and can separate that need from a taxable event—for example, being forced to sell capital gains in a down market.

Investment positions that have been held for a long period of time and have built up big capital gains create liquidity challenges for their owners. Selling can create a huge taxable event. Owners may end up holding positions that should have been sold long ago, just because the owners don't want to pay the capital gains taxes. They end up holding positions permanently with no access to liquidity.

If you own highly appreciated securities, you might be a candidate for using an SBLOC account to unlock access to funds without experiencing a taxable event.

Using an SBLOC, you can leave your securities invested, borrow against the value of your nonqualified investment portfolio, and use a tax-free loan to generate proceeds for whatever cash flow need you may have.

Back when we had lower-than-historical interest rates, you could potentially expect to hold these loans for years. Now that we are having record-high interest rates, these types of loans have become less attractive. Fortunately, you can elect for a fixed or variable interest rate, so that if and when interest rates come down again, then so would the interest rate on your variable interest rate SBLOC account.

You can collateralize your SBLOC account with equities or fixed income, and some lenders will allow cash and cash equivalents. When you set up your SBLOC account, it is a demand loan, so there is no maturity date.

Typically, you can borrow 50% to 60% of the value of a diversified investment portfolio. These loans require interest payments every month; they can be made via ACH from your bank account. As for loan principal, this can be repaid at any time via ACH or check. There is no prepayment penalty.

If you're wondering what it takes to set up one of these accounts, you must complete an online application and provide a copy of your photo ID and a recent investment account statement. They will generally send you loan documents via digital delivery. You can also set up an online account to monitor your application status and loan portfolio details.

Similar to highly appreciated real estate, a nonqualified investment account invested in stocks and bonds can potentially benefit from the step-up in basis tax laws available when someone dies. This is where the SBLOC, like the 1031 exchange, can allow an investor to defer the capital gain until they die. Unlike the 1031 exchange, the SBLOC can provide some tax-free cash flow to the owners when needed on demand during their life.

In community property states, when the investment account is properly titled in a revocable living trust account holding assets as community property with rights of survivorship, at the passing of the first spouse, the surviving spouse will receive a full step-up in basis.

You can enjoy access to tax-free loan proceeds from your SBLOC, and then receive a full step-up in basis at the passing of the first spouse. At this time, it looks like the step-up in basis tax laws may now be maintained for some time, even though President Biden tried to do away with the step-up in basis rules back in 2021.

Costs, Risks, and Considerations for the SBLOC

- Interest rates can be fixed or variable. Interest must be paid monthly. It is a demand loan, so there are no prepayment penalties, and the lender can demand that the loan must be repaid at any time.
- You could be subject to increased borrowing costs with the current higher interest rates.
- Your securities in your investment portfolio are subject to market risk, and if they should drop too far in a market downturn, you could be subject to a collateral call. You could be forced to sell positions or raise more collateral to make up the difference.
- Lenders may impose several limitations on the assets within the account.
- Because an SBLOC will generally loan you more than a margin account, it may be riskier than a margin account because

they have given you more access to your equity.

- There are no additional fees, points, or closing costs for a non-purpose loan (SBLOC).
- If you pay the loan off, the credit line will normally remain open and available.

When we consider SBLOCs, they offer another potential source of tax-free cash flow. You don't pay any taxes, your spouse does not pay any taxes, and the kids don't pay any capital gains tax, because of the step-up in basis at the death of the surviving spouse.

Essentially, this is another tax-free tool that you can use to potentially avoid capital gains taxes altogether.

Health Savings Accounts (HSAs)

Health savings accounts (HSAs) are a great tax tool. When you contribute to an HSA on the front end, it's similar to a traditional IRA in that you get a tax deduction. And then, while the money is invested, it gets to grow tax-deferred—it's growing, and you're not paying taxes on the growth annually. Then the magic begins. If you pull it out and use it for qualified medical expenses, it comes out income tax–free.

A tax deduction on the front end, tax-deferred growth while you invest, and tax-free distributions to pay for qualified medical expenses in retirement—that's a phenomenal tax-free tool.

Considerations with HSAs

- In order to participate in and have an HSA account, you must have a high-deductible health insurance plan.

- There is a 20% tax penalty for early (under age 65) nonmedical withdrawals from the plan. This is a stiff penalty. So don't do it.

- If you are on Medicare, you cannot contribute to an HSA. If you do, the contributions are subject to a 6% "excess contributions" excise tax penalty. This applies to a six-month look back if you sign up for Medicare past age 65.

- After age 65 or if you become disabled, you can withdraw HSA funds without penalty, but proceeds must be used for medical expenses, or they will be subject to ordinary income tax.

529 Plans

529 plan benefits can vary depending on the state. I'll focus on Arizona, since I know that state so intimately.

If you're a married couple (MFJ) in Arizona, you can take up to a $4,000 state income tax deduction against your Arizona income taxes for a contribution to a 529 plan in any calendar year. You put your money in, you get a tax deduction, and the money grows tax-deferred.

If the beneficiary uses the funds for qualified expenses such as tuition, books, computers, internet, software—basically everything for school and education—the money comes out income tax–free to the beneficiary.

I have a number of clients who use 529 plans to save for their grandchildren's education. Many clients steadily fund the accounts each year for each of their grandchildren. The goal is to get to the point where each account has enough in it to fund college fully. The amount of that goal is different for each family.

There is some flexibility with 529 plans as well. Let's say your child or grandchild grows up, and instead of going to college, they go straight into the workforce.

If you have another beneficiary, another child or grandchild whose education you wish to fund instead, you could transfer the beneficiary designation to the other child.

You could also use a 529 plan to fund continuing education for yourself—for instance, if you wanted to attend golf school. Or, if you wanted to pull the money out for yourself, you could do so with a 10% penalty.

After the passing of the SECURE Act 2.0 at the end of 2022, 529 plans have become even better tax-free tools. The Consolidated Appropriations Act of 2023 will allow beneficiaries of 529 plans beginning in 2024 to roll over up to $35,000 aggregate over their lifetime from a 529 account to a Roth IRA. The rollover amounts are subject to the annual Roth IRA contribution limits, and the 529 account must have been open for more than 15 years to qualify for this benefit. This will allow families to plan for bigger 529 plans with the assurance that any "leftover" 529 funds will be put to good use and can avoid taxes or penalties if rolled over to a Roth IRA account for the benefit of the 529 beneficiary.

Risks, Penalties, and Considerations with 529 Plans

If you withdraw the funds and do not use them for qualified education expenses, you will have to pay both federal income tax and a 10% penalty on the growth/earnings in the account. Depending on your state, the growth could be subject to state income tax as well.

Harvesting Gains and Harvesting Losses—Do Both!

Much like harvesting gains, if you invest in something and sell it while it's down, you can harvest that loss to offset capital gains somewhere else or in a future tax year when you will need losses to offset your gains that year.

If a married couple filing jointly has an income around $94,050, and they have harvested some losses, their income could be further lowered. If they have taxable investments that have traded up in value, and they sell them, they could have up to that $94,050 in income and capital gains and the tax rate on the capital gains will be zero. That's right: *zero*.

If they own a business or enterprise where the business posts a big loss that year—maybe they had a loss of, say, $50,000—they could essentially harvest gains from their investment accounts with taxable income of $110,000 and still qualify for a 0% capital gains tax on some capital gains due to the business loss.

People generally don't think about actually selling gains as a tax move, but determining your situation each year with an annual tax plan can help you take advantage of the opportunity to harvest gains and losses.

The Two-Generation Tax-Free Legacy Plan™

Let me ask you two important questions.

1. Have you accumulated enough wealth that it is likely that you will leave an inheritance to your children when you and your spouse pass away?

2. Given the choice, would you rather leave your children a lump sum inheritance that may or may not be taxable, or would you prefer to leave them a portion of their inheritance as an asset-protected, tax-free income stream for life?

I have found that many people don't necessarily want to leave all their legacy money to their children in one big lump sum. They would love to leave a portion of their legacy to their children as a tax-free income stream that their children can use for decades. Knowing that the future income tax rates in the United States are likely headed much higher, they want to seek a way to leave tax-free income to their children, rather than just a big lump sum.

The Two-Generation Tax-Free Legacy Plan™ aims to provide the desired legacy benefits that many of us hope to provide for our children. A legacy plan that can potentially provide tax-free income that is asset protected and will provide tax-free income for the entire life of your children and then hopefully leave a tax-free inheritance for your grandchildren as well.

The goal of this strategy is to provide a tax-free income stream for the rest of your child's life. You see, instead of just providing a big lump sum, at death, many parents desire to leave a legacy with a long-term plan to provide a tax-free income benefit to help protect their children from the higher tax rates of the future.

This strategy is not common knowledge in the industry as it combines tax law, retirement plan rules, trust law, investment regulations, insurance regulations, and estate tax law regulations.

I am the creator and founder of this strategy. I am introducing it to the world with this book. It is my intellectual property. So, I obviously cannot provide you with all the details in this medium. I want to make sure that it is used correctly, so I am licensing it to qualified and licensed professionals, so they can work as a team to provide the strategy to you. If you would like to learn more so you can implement this strategy for your family, please reach out to us at movingtotaxfree.com, and we will put you in touch with a team that will be able to help you implement this strategy for yourself. It is not a perfect fit for everyone and is not available for everyone. The professionals that we guide you to will be able to evaluate your situation and see if you qualify and if the strategy will be a beneficial fit for your situation.

CHAPTER 11

APPLYING THE TAX BRACKET STRATEGY

It May Feel Painful in the Process, but the Tax Bracket Strategy Will Be Worth It for You and Your Family Over the Long Term

"Always plan ahead. It wasn't raining when Noah built the ark."

—PROVERB

Now that we've covered tips and tools for the move to tax-free, I want to share a practical application of the tax bracket strategy.

Let's use the example of a retired couple, Jim and Jen.[66] Jim used to work as an executive in the tech industry. He was at the top of the pile in terms of earnings. Jim and Jen were smart with their money. They saved diligently for years and years, and Jim fully funded his 401(k), so as a couple they have a healthy pile of money for their retirement.

They are about one-third of the way through a 10-year process of

---

66 .I've adjusted a few of the couple's details to obscure their identity, but the examples of their taxes are accurate.

converting their traditional IRAs to Roth IRAs—they're converting $300,000 or so each year.

They have one daughter, and they want to provide for her and for their grandchildren with tax-free money when they eventually pass away.

Effective Tax Rate Parfait

As I noted previously, taxes are broken down by marginal and effective tax rates. Your marginal tax rate reflects the tax rate you will pay on your last dollar of income, while your effective tax rate represents the percentage of tax you will pay averaged across all your income for the year. Your first earnings are not taxed—the tax rate at that point is zero—and then, as your taxable income increases, the tax rate jumps to 10%, then 12%, then 22%, then 24%, then 32%, then 35%, and then 37%. These are the tax brackets for 2024.

Think of the effective tax rate as a parfait. There's the Jell-O on the bottom, then a creamy middle section, then whipped cream, and maybe chopped fruit on the top. When you dip your spoon into the parfait and get a little bit of each section in a bite, that's your effective tax rate. Starting at the bottom as your income fills up that tax bracket amount, your next dollars of income will spill over into the next higher tax bracket as your income increases, until you max out at your highest marginal tax rate for your last dollars of income for that year.

With Jim and Jen's tax planning, the biggest variable is their taxable IRA to Roth IRA conversion each year.

Their baseline income (which includes dividends, capital gains, taxable pensions and annuities, IRA RMD, and taxable Social Security benefits) is roughly $100,000 each year. The fluctuation with their AGI, and subsequently their effective tax rate, depends on the amount that we convert to a Roth IRA each year.

The Sweet Spot

The key to effectively using the tax bracket strategy is understanding how much money to convert to a tax-free vehicle (a Roth IRA or a LIRP) each year—and recognizing how that conversion will impact the effective tax rate.

For year one, Jim and Jen's adjusted gross income was $430,000, about $320,000 of which was from a Roth IRA conversion. That year, they ended up with a marginal tax rate of 32% but an effective tax rate of 21.7%.

They ended up owing about $85,000 in taxes.

For the second year, we ran multiple projections based on the amount of their Roth IRA conversion. If they converted about $200,000 from their IRA to a Roth IRA, their AGI would wind up at about $325,000, with an effective tax rate of 20%.

If they decided to shift about $285,000 from their IRA to a Roth IRA, their AGI would wind up just above $400,000, with an effective tax rate of about 22%.

If they converted $360,000 to a Roth IRA, their AGI would jump to about $480,000 and they would have an effective tax rate of about 24%.

If they converted $585,000 to a Roth IRA, their AGI would rise to over $700,000, with a marginal tax rate of 37%—and an effective tax rate of 27.7%.

Digging Deeper

Let's focus a little bit more on the conversion of $360,000. True, they would have to pay nearly $116,000 in taxes for the year. But the effective tax rate would only be 24%, even though they would be converting so much more money.

For married couples filing jointly in the tax year (2023) of this projection, a marginal tax rate of 24%—the tax rate of your final dollar—reached $326,600, so only their next dollars of Roth IRA above that amount would be taxed at 32%, up to $414,700, then 35% to $622,050, and 37% for anything above that.

What I want to teach you is to focus on the effective tax rate. We don't want you to jump into the higher marginal tax rates with too much income, but even if you dip into those higher marginal tax rates, an effective tax rate of 22% to 24% is ideal when you have so much money invested in tax-deferred IRAs and you need to get it moved to tax-free Roth IRAs. In 2024 the 24% marginal tax bracket for couples filing MFJ will allow you to have taxable income of $383,900 and still stay in the 24% tax bracket.

With these projections, the goal is to use the tax brackets and money sources to see how large of a conversion you can make while keeping the effective tax rate as low as possible—but also making sure that you are converting your IRAs and 401(k)s in a reasonable amount of time. If someone has $3 million in a traditional IRA, and they're only converting $50,000 a year, they're not going to get the money converted in any reasonable amount of time. It will take them the rest of their life. In fact, the growth in the account may be more than they are converting in any given year. They may be going backward.

But if they were converting $300,000 each year, they could reposition the money to tax-free in roughly 10 years.

This process is all about using strategic intent each and every year to reposition your tax-deferred and taxable accounts to tax-free accounts. It may feel painful in the process, but I truly believe it will be worth it for you and your family over the long term.

Making the Tax Payment

The best way to pay the taxes for this process is to use taxable money from a taxable brokerage account or regular savings account. If you use the money in the IRA to pay taxes, then there is less money available to be converted to a Roth IRA account in future years.

I meet with a lot of retired clients who have $2 or $3 million in IRAs or 401(k)s and wonder how they're ever going to get their money converted—and many don't really have that much other taxable money saved up. Their nest egg is in their 401(k) that they saved for all those years. In those cases, we can take a distribution from the IRA and push it directly to the federal and state governments to pay the taxes.

In these cases, we may not be able to convert as much because some of the traditional IRA that would be used to convert to a Roth will have to be diverted to pay the federal and state taxes. We are still trying to manage the tax bracket, and so we will send some of the money to the taxing authorities to pay the income tax. There is a nuance, though.

We can hold off on making that tax payment from the traditional IRA to the feds and to the state until later in the year. You can let that account grow all year, get almost a full year's additional growth on the IRA, and then toward the end of the year, pay the taxes out of that traditional account. We usually pay those tax payments for our clients directly from the IRA in November each year. It's such an easy process. There are no stamps, no envelopes, and no checks to mail. People *hate* writing checks for federal taxes.

This can cover the requirements for estimated taxes for the client as well, so instead of making estimated tax payments, we can pay the taxes toward the end of the year from the traditional IRA account. This helps lower the amount that we will need to convert to a Roth IRA for those people with large IRA accounts. This is a very popular way to make the Roth IRA conversion process easier to tolerate each year—paying the taxes from the traditional IRA account that is already infested with taxes.

The Bottom Line

Let's take that $2 million that Jim and Jen have left in their traditional IRA. If it stayed there for 10 years with a 7% growth rate each year, the IRA would grow to about $4 million (using the rule of 72) before their child would be required to pull the money out and pay taxes. Of that $4 million, the taxes might be 37%—that's about $1.5

million gone to Uncle Sam right off the bat *if they're lucky.* And then another 4% or 5% for the state. They're probably looking at losing $1.7 million just like that.

Almost 85% of the growth would be lost to taxes. And maybe more than that if future tax rates are as high as we fear from the experts' predictions.

On the other hand, if the IRA were converted to a Roth IRA, the same $2 million account, after taxes were paid from the account, could potentially grow to $2.96 million in a Roth IRA (using the rule of 72). That additional savings will go a long way in taking care of their daughter and grandchildren.

Tax Bracket Strategy—Step by Step

- Step 1: Create a forward-looking tax plan. (This will require you to have tax-planning software or a tax professional to help you.) Consider your taxable income before a Roth conversion, and then again at different amounts that you may want to convert (e.g., $50,000, $100,000, $150,000, $200,000).
- Step 2: Consider what each additional amount of Roth IRA conversion will do to your tax rate. Look at both marginal and effective tax rates. (Marginal tax rate is the rate at which the next dollar will be taxed. Effective tax rate is the actual tax rate [percentage] you will pay on all the taxable income.)
- Step 3: Make note of the marginal tax rates in 2024. The best tax bracket, in my opinion, that you would want to fill is the 24% tax bracket. (This will be about $383,900 in taxable income for married couples filing jointly (MFJ).) The next high-

er marginal tax rate is 32%, 8% higher, and may be too high.

- Step 4: Consider the unintended consequences of the Roth conversion. Look at the costs (e.g., making your Social Security benefits taxable, pushing your income high enough that you become subject to Medicare IRMAA penalties) and weigh them to see if it is still worth it. Look up what those penalties are, and consider if it is more important and beneficial to you to get the IRA moved into a tax-free Roth IRA. I like to look at the penalties as additional taxes. If you calculate them as a tax rate, usually you will find it is still worthwhile to move forward converting your tax-deferred accounts to the tax-free Roth IRA.

CHAPTER 12

INFLATION—THE HIDDEN TAX

One Form of Tax Isn't Like the Others

"By a continuing process of inflation, governments can confis-cate, secretly and unobserved, an important part of the wealth of their citizens."

—JOHN MAYNARD KEYNES[67]

One form of tax isn't like the others.

In 2022, the inflation rate in the United States reached 8.5%, the highest it's been in 40 years.[68] That inflation, unfortunately, is a tax—a hidden stealth tax.

We can control the amount of federal and state income taxes we pay by making the move to tax-free investment vehicles. We can attempt to control our investments, and if we manage those properly,

---

67 John Maynard Keynes, *The Economic Consequences of the Peace* (New York: Harcourt Brace Jovanovich, 1920), 235–48.

68 Paul Wiseman, Anne D'Innocenzio, and Mae Anderson, "U.S. Inflation Jumped 8.5% in Past Year, Highest Since 1981," April 12, 2022, https://apnews.com/article/us-inflation-rate-historic-high-4ba3435cc3730198e299690a9d968038.

the hope is that they can grow as fast as, or faster than, inflation. But you and I cannot control our inflation rate.

Inflation is a tax on everybody—it's a tax on the spending power of the American dollar, and it reflects how far a dollar will take us now compared to one, or five, or even 10 years from now.

The inflation tax affects lower-income people disproportionately more than it affects the wealthy—the wealthy can more easily afford to pay more. Inflation is terrible because there's no going back; it's not as if we're ever going to go backward and prices are ever going to move significantly lower in the future. Just try and take cost of living adjustments from workers or from Social Security beneficiaries. Wage inflation tends to creep higher but never seems to go back down again. Inflation confiscates your standard of living as expenses explode higher, consuming your ability to keep up.

As of this writing, the Fed is trying to tamp down inflation by raising interest rates. In early 2022, we were almost at a 0.08% fed funds rate. And by the end of December 2022, the fed funds rate had shot up to 4.33%. In February 2024 our fed funds rate had hit 5.5%.[69]

That is the fastest increase in interest rates that we've seen, perhaps ever. The rate of change of the interest rates hasn't been fully felt yet—we're only beginning to see the effects of that rate change.

Where Inflation Is Being Felt

Inflation is felt in everything we do—filling up a tank of gas, buy-

---

69　"Federal Funds Effective Rate," FRED Economic Data, accessed May 1, 2023, https://fred.stlouisfed.org/series/FEDFUNDS.

ing plane tickets, and going to the grocery store. What used to be a pound of bacon is now one-fourth of a pound, and yet it costs twice as much as it used to. Inflation is going out to dinner for a hamburger and fries and getting a bill for $42 and wondering where your money went—when the same meal a few years ago would have cost you $20 to $25.

Where inflation is really being felt is the real estate market. Construction has come to a screeching halt. Progress has slowed due to supply shortages and project overruns. Employers are having to raise wages to keep pace with inflation—but that also means raising rates for customers, which leaves business owners caught in this conundrum of margin squeeze.

Ripple Effects

That hidden tax of inflation causes so many other ripple effects across the economy. Employee wages have to increase in order to provide for the inflation these workers are having to deal with.

Because the interest rates have moved up so fast, we saw fixed income accounts such as mutual funds and bonds losing 15% to 20% in 2022. That's in addition to the S&P 500 being down 20%.

People witnessed a good portion of their investments evaporate in just one year.

Higher inflation rates reinforce the need to use a "buckets of money" approach for your retirement planning, investing your near-term money needed for current income in safer stable value investments and your longer-term money in longer-term investment vehicles that can keep up with and beat these higher inflation rates.

If you can't stomach the thought of investing in the equity markets without any downside protection, new investment vehicles like buffered ETFs can provide you with "downside buffer protection" on the first 15% (20% is also available) if the markets should trade down during the year. If the markets trade below the buffer, you can and will lose value dollar for dollar with the drop in the market below the buffer protection level.

So, if the market drops 15% or less in the next year, at the end of the year, the account will true your balance back up to zero, and you will not have lost anything. This can potentially give you, the investor, the confidence to have staying power and not panic by pulling your money out at exactly the wrong time, when the market is down. You need to allocate a large enough portion of your investments into asset classes that can keep up with, and perhaps stay ahead of, inflation. If you don't, your retirement income nest egg can be consumed by the stealth tax of inflation—even if you have moved to tax-free.

Factoring in Inflation

In moving to tax-free, the inflation rate per se is not part of the calculation.

With our financial planning software, we typically apply a long-term inflation rate. Historically, we've used 3%. Going forward, that may not be enough.

Inflation can certainly slow the economy down. There'll be companies that have a hard time making money when the interest rates are so high, which means that they can't borrow as much, and they can't grow as fast.

We'll see if 3% over a 30-year period of retirement is enough, but it might have to be raised to 4% or 5%. With our financial planning software, we can easily illustrate the different inflation rates. We've had clients who came in and said, "I want you to illustrate what my portfolio looks like with a 4% or 5% inflation rate." They want to know that they'll still be OK in retirement, even with a higher inflation rate.

The right financial planning software is extremely helpful in demonstrating, with just a few clicks, what someone's future could look like with different inflation rates applied.

They can see how inflation will impact their planning and whether they could run out of money. Those insights can influence their decision to take a little bit more risk on their longer-term investments in order to achieve a higher rate of return so that they're OK over the long term.

"Have I saved enough money?" That's a question everyone needs to answer. If someone has saved a big enough pile of money, they don't have to take a lot of risk with their investments. But if the pile isn't big enough, or you're not sure if it is, then that's a different matter altogether.

Those who are conservative by nature may need to invest more aggressively than they typically would feel comfortable with.

What you don't know…*can* hurt you. How can you know how you should be investing your life's savings in order to be OK in retirement?

We can create a financial plan using sophisticated financial planning software and tell a person with a high degree of confidence, "It looks like you'll potentially run out of money at age 85 with your current level of spending, inflation, and income."

That might be fine if they die at 82, but what if they live until 92? Living from age 82 to age 92 without any money is not a situation that I want any of you in.

This illustrates the importance of having a professional financial plan prepared and updated each year to make sure you are on track to be OK and not run out of money, either because you had to pay too much of it in taxes, or you overspent based on your retirement savings, or inflation ate your retirement savings and put your standard of living in peril.

The Importance of Financial Planning

If your income needs are going up by 4% or 5% each year, instead of 2% or 3%, in order to keep up with inflation, it's crucial that you take the steps necessary to protect your income from the inflation we are experiencing.

Social Security beneficiaries received an 8.7% cost of living increase in 2023 for their Social Security benefits based on the inflation experienced in 2022. That alone may not be enough in the face of the inflation we are currently facing as a country. You will likely need to find investment strategies that can provide you with the growth you need in your portfolio, while at the same time offering downside protection for your investments.

If you've done the planning to become income tax–free, your Social Security benefits are potentially not taxable and your other income is likely not taxable as well.

With higher inflation since 2022, you will have to be able to generate more income in your tax-free portfolios in order to maintain your standard of living and keep up with the higher inflation it looks like we may face going forward into the 2020s and 2030s.

CHAPTER 13

CONTROLLABLES AND UNCONTROLLABLES

There Are Lots of Unknowns, Including the Future Tax Rates

"You can only control what you can control."

—HEATHER O'REILLY

These days when I meet with people, I ask how they're doing. You can sense a weight on their shoulders, an uneasiness. Things are difficult. They're worried about the way the world is headed. They are worried about the path we're on in this country and in the world. They are very concerned and know that things can't continue the way they are without disastrous consequences in the future.

Here are some of the things I hear that people are worrying about:

- The banks. Silicon Valley Bank just went bankrupt in 2023.
- Inflation.
- Higher interest rates.
- The markets. In 2022, the S&P lost 18.11%, and the bond market (AGG) was down 13%. When both markets are down

at the same time, people worry.

- Immigration, drugs, crime, and personal and national security.
- The war in Ukraine.
- Threats from China, Iran, North Korea, and Russia.
- Oil, gas, and the prices of those commodities.
- Our national debt and the financial challenges to Social Security and Medicare.
- The political division in our country.

All of these and many more are areas of concern that are on all of our minds.

These are variables we cannot control. And it's important to take stock of them.

Who Will Be in Charge at the Federal or State Level of Government?

Different government leaders have different approaches to spending and taxes. And in today's hyperpartisan climate, it's tough to project who might have political power in the future and how their approach could impact tax rates. No matter who is in control, we feel confident that taxes will be raised significantly in the future. You may find yourself paying more taxes sooner depending on who's in political office.

Capital Gains Taxes

On multiple occasions, President Biden's administration has proposed increasing capital gains taxes, including one scenario that saw them rising as high as 39.6%[70] (That proposal was scrapped in 2021.) Then again, in his 2023 budget, he wanted to treat capital gains taxes as ordinary income and raise the tax rate to 39.6%. The Biden administration also floated the possibility of terminating the step-up in basis rules in 2021 and was considering this again in 2023. The step-up in basis rules are a great cleansing tool for tax-accounting purposes. They allow families to clean up the tracking of basis on real estate and other holdings that might not have been maintained for decades.

Imagine that your grandfather bought a piece of real property back in the 1950s or 1960s, when records were typed up on a type-writer and there were not any photocopies or digital copies.

Imagine further all the improvements that have been made over the years to that property. Can you imagine the nightmare of trying to go back and reconstruct the costs incurred on all those records after your grandfather has passed away? He is not available to answer your questions, and you must now somehow re-create the cost basis yourself. Or you can just pay the capital gains tax and depreciation recapture tax on all of it. That would be a tax bloodbath for your family. I am sure you can imagine the nightmare that this could become.

I feel confident that, now that it has been proposed once, this wonderful tax loophole will be taken away someday in the future. Until then, be sure to fully take advantage of the step-up in basis tax rules. You won't be able to control the day this rule will be changed.

---

70   Kelley R. Taylor, "Biden Calls for Doubling of Capital Gains Tax Rate," Kiplinger, last updated March 10, 2023, https://www.kiplinger.com/taxes/biden-calls-for-doubling-capital-gains-tax-rate.

Future Tax Rates

The biggest uncontrollable, of course, is the future tax rates.

My wife Laura and I took a trip to Monaco and Italy in 2019. Monaco is actually the second-smallest country in the world, and all the rich and famous flock to Monaco. Why? Because it's a tax-free haven. We had a black-car driver take us back and forth from the airport. We used an Italian driver over in Italy to help us see all the tourist sights in Rome.

I was curious, and I had a few questions for the drivers about their pay and the taxes they paid to France and to Italy (to visit Monaco, you fly into Nice, France). They both told me that they earn about 100,000 euros per year and that their tax rate is 65%. That leaves them with about 35,000 euros to live on.

That tax rate might sound ridiculous, but it is the reality right now in Europe. Sure, they have nationalized health care. But that hardly seems like a worthwhile trade.

A Look Overseas

For a good preview of what's ahead, consider the top income tax rates in these foreign countries:

European OECD Country	Top Statutory Personal Income Tax Rate
Austria (AT)	55.0%
Belgium (BE)	53.5%
Czech Republic (CZ)	23.0%

European OECD Country	Top Statutory Personal Income Tax Rate
Denmark (DK)	55.9%
Estonia (EE)	20.0%
Finland (FI)	51.2%
France (FR)	55.4%
Germany (DE)	47.5%
Greece (GR)	54.0%
Hungary (HU)	15.0%
Iceland (IS)	46.2%
Ireland (IE)	48.0%
Italy (IT)	47.2%
Latvia (LV)	31.0%
Lithuania (LT)	32.0%
Luxembourg (LU)	45.8%
Netherlands (NL)	49.5%
Norway (NO)	39.4%
Poland (PL)	36.0%
Portugal (PT)	53.0%
Slovakia (SK)	25.0%
Slovenia (SI)	50.0%
Spain (ES)	54.0%
Sweden (SE)	52.3%
Switzerland (CH)	44.8%
Turkey (TR)	40.8%
United Kingdom (GB)	45.0%

Source: PwC, "Worldwide Tax Summaries," accessed Feb. 1, 2022, taxsummaries.pwc.co.[71]

---

71 Daniel Bunn, "Top Personal Income Tax Rates in Europe," Tax Foundation, February 8, 2022, https://taxfoundation.org/top-personal-income-tax-rates-europe-2022/.

Suddenly, our top tax rate of 37% doesn't seem all that bad!

The Tax Foundation reports that the average income tax rate in 2020 was just 13.6%. The top 1% of taxpayers paid an average rate of about 26%.[72]

This means there is still room for U.S. taxpayers to pay income tax rates in line with the rest of the world.

In the years ahead, the tax rates here in America are bound to rise and follow the direction of the tax rates in Europe.

I recently met with some clients about using up the 24% tax bracket using a Roth conversion. Think about it. We are increasing their tax rate with a Roth conversion and arriving at a final effective tax rate of 24%. David Walker has indicated that tax rates will most likely have to double in the United States. That means future tax rates will have to rise to more like 45% to 50%. Do you think the American people are prepared for what's coming?

Are *you* prepared for what's coming?

I see Europe's tax rates as a preview of where the United States is headed. We're not there yet—and a big reason why is because the United States holds the reserve currency of the world. So, we are bingeing right now on debt. We are printing money to fund our annual budget—to the tune of more than $1.5 trillion per year![73]

I'm not getting political here—this is a situation created by Re-

72 Erica York, "Summary of the Latest Federal Income Tax Data, 2023 Update," Tax Foundation, January 26, 2023, https://taxfoundation.org/publications/latest-federal-income-tax-data/.

73 "Guide to the Markets," J.P. Morgan, February 28, 2023, https://am.jpmorgan.com/us/en/asset-management/adv/insights/market-insights/guide-to-the-markets/.

publicans and Democrats alike.

When that moment of truth arrives, the moment when our tax rates have to rise to the same rates as the rest of the world, and we are no longer able to fund our future by printing more money, the American people are going to be in for a shock of unimaginable proportions.

The one thing we can control, by converting our money from a tax-deferred untaxed traditional IRA to a tax-free Roth, is the tax rate on that nest egg. By moving to tax-free now, no matter how high the future tax rates go, you have controlled the tax rate on your nest egg. Because you have already paid the tax, and you have controlled the tax rate at which you paid that tax.

This future tax burden is going to be piled on our children and grandchildren. They are going to be paying for it for a very long time. Here's the opportunity for those of you who educate yourselves and are willing to tolerate delayed gratification.

You are going to leave your family in a much better place than those who follow along with the "sheeple" and get sheared by the government plan.

For a lot of younger readers—those in their twenties, thirties, and forties—if you can contribute to a Roth IRA or a Roth 401(k), you're going to be so much further ahead of your peers.

When you're young and healthy, the cost of insurance is so much less expensive. Those who can invest $5,000, $10,000, or $20,000 per year—or even more than that, like $75,000 or $100,000 per year—toward their LIRP and do that for 20 or 30 or 40 years will see a monumental difference from those who grow their money and then have to pay taxes later, potentially at a much higher rate.

Rising Interest Rates

As I noted earlier, interest rates increased dramatically during 2022 at a rate we haven't seen in 40-plus years. The impacts of that change aren't fully clear yet, but they've already started to have an impact on the housing market.

Supply Chain Shortages

Supply chain issues became more prevalent during the COVID-19 pandemic, which was itself another uncontrollable. These issues have led to backlogs and backups, which have reduced consumer confidence while making goods more expensive, and they have caused increased costs that have been left to the customer to cover.

Inflation

Inflation has become rampant, and that inflation is only giving people more anxiety and concern. It worries them that things are going to cost more—and with taxes set to rise and inflation spiking, that combination creates urgency in them to want to do something. To act.

Because while people can control their taxes to some degree, they can't control inflation.

Focusing on the Controllables

It's important to recognize that we can't control uncontrollable issues.

The controllables are bound to come and go, and some will become major issues affecting our lives dramatically. But, by the same token, if we realize that we cannot control the uncontrollables, it offers us peace of mind to focus on the things that *are* within our power to control. Spiraling inflation and lingering pandemic and recession fears only confirm the importance of controlling the controllables. You can't control inflation or the devaluation of your dollar, but you do have some control over your future tax rates and retirement, and so you should take control wherever and however you can.

Controlling the Uncontrollables

I sent a letter to my clients in October of 2022. Normally, we use low-cost mutual funds and ETFs for investment vehicles to achieve the asset allocation and diversification goals we seek for our clients. The problem was that late in 2022, I couldn't find an allocation I wanted to make using mutual funds or ETFs. There was not a manager who did everything that I wanted to do.

We ended up creating a custom stock portfolio to combat what was going on in the world: inflation; rising interest rates (not just in the U.S. but around the world); the war in Ukraine; shortages of oil, gas, natural gas, and diesel; rising medical and pharmaceutical expenses; lingering effects of COVID-19; supply chain shortages; and the coming slowdown that's already apparent in the real estate market.

Those are all things we can't control.

But using a new stock portfolio, I wanted to invest in energy; I wanted to be in fertilizer and phosphates because 40% of the world's supply comes from two mines, one in Ukraine, one in Russia, that were offline during the war. I wanted to be invested in biotech, health care, and pharma because they had all been defensive and profitable over the course of the year in 2022, when the S&P 500 was down about 20% for the year.

I wanted to be invested in the defense stocks because our supplies in the United States have been depleted supplying the war in Ukraine. And Lockheed Martin and Northrop Grumman and other companies like them are making good money, and they're going to continue to make money going forward. I wanted a little bit of bank finances since, as interest rates go higher, they're going to be able to make more money. I wanted food companies because everybody has to have food and the prices are rising. Those companies are making money and are profitable, and they will be able to maintain their profit margins. I wanted some best-of-class retail like Costco—if you ever go into a Costco, it's always busy.

There's no other retailer except for possibly Amazon that can give Costco a run for its money.

You can control your investment allocation. You might not be able to control the uncontrollables, but you can act and react to them with your controllables in order to navigate the craziness in this world.

I went through this exercise to let you know that the world has changed; you cannot continue to invest in just a 60/40 mix and never make any changes to your portfolio. In 2022, the S&P 500 was down about 19.4%. The Barclays AGG index, which represents the intermediate bond market, was down about 15% in 2022.

I don't know about you, but that does not feel like an acceptable result for the year. Yes, the markets are going to have some down years. But when both bonds and stocks are down at the same time, you have to consider doing something different going forward, as the Federal Reserve continues to raise interest rates in the face of inflation.

This example represents my approach at one specific moment in time—and that approach can shift and change based on the facts and circumstances of you, the client. I shared this example not so you can replicate my process, but so you can see the type of effort a financial planner should make in terms of capitalizing on opportunities and adjusting based on trends and patterns. If your experts are sitting idly by, continuing to hold your money in losing assets without being proactive about market trends, it might be time for you to start looking for a new advisor.

The Necessary Adjustments

Even though inflation is uncontrollable, as taxpayers or investors, we have ways to ameliorate some of the impacts of inflation. We can adjust our spending. As an example, if you like to travel, with the higher cost of airline tickets, you might choose to travel less.

With food prices higher, you might be more selective about what you eat and how much you eat out.

The rising interest rates are definitely having an impact on the housing market. If someone owns their home with a 2.5% mortgage, guess what—they're not going anywhere. With mortgage interest rates up as high as 6.3% to 8%, the math does not support people selling and buying another home. Real estate values will likely drop due to the lowered activity caused by the higher mortgage interest rates.

Opportunities and Potholes

The uncontrollables will cause us to adjust. But there are ways we can prepare.

Take, for instance, the time during the height of the COVID-19 pandemic when people were stocking up on toilet paper. If you already had plentiful supplies of toilet paper, guess what? Inflation on toilet paper didn't affect you.

My job is to find places and opportunities to make money for my clients—to predict the opportunities and potholes in the road ahead.

Conventional wisdom suggests that you should stay invested long term and ride the market up and down. That it's not worth trying to out-pick or outperform the market long term.

I agree with that science on a basic level. The problem is that the science is based on the average over a very long period of time, and it has been measured over a period of time where the Fed has been stimulative to the markets, holding interest rates lower over the last 40 years (since 1981).

But the environment has changed, and the Fed is no longer holding interest rates down. This is not a normal time—and conventional wisdom has to be thrown out the window because, as demonstrated, normal markets were not the case in 2022, as the Fed raised interest rates at an unprecedented pace.

This is a good reminder that investment choices can definitely make a difference. No, we can't have 20/20 vision on everything. But you can see supply chain issues and oil shortages around the world, in addition to the war in Ukraine, and it doesn't take a brain surgeon to figure out the way things are headed.

The Biggest Potholes

One of the first potholes that my clients have to worry about is long-term care.

Remember, my generation, the baby boomers, are like a rat going through a snake—all those postwar babies are in their sixties and seventies now and retiring.

According to Health and Human Services, there's a 70% chance that those 65 or older will need some type of long-term care services.[74]

Now, if you invest in the right kind of permanent life insurance retirement plan, the policy will include, at no additional charge, a chronic care rider or a living benefit rider, which will allow you to accelerate the death benefit, take it out, and use it for long-term care, without you having to die to receive this benefit. This means that you can get access to the death benefit while you're alive, and you can use

---

74 "How Much Care Will You Need?," LongTermCare.gov, last modified February 18, 2020, https://acl.gov/ltc/basic-needs/how-much-care-will-you-need.

it for your own long-term care needs.

With an asset-based long-term care policy, not a traditional long-term care policy, the insurance company can never raise the premiums, and you pay a set amount for a set period of time, and then the policy is paid in full. Long-term care is one of the big potholes that the baby boomer generation will face. If you don't insure for this risk, you are assuming the risk. Some people can afford to self-insure, but even if that is the case, I find many wealthy people who, knowing the odds, would rather be sure that their long-term needs are insured.

If you are assuming this risk, you could be putting your spouse or yourself in a compromised situation if one of you experiences an extended long-term care requirement.

What if one of the spouses gets Alzheimer's and has to go into a memory care unit? Those can cost hundreds of dollars each day; many such facilities are running $10,000 to $12,000 per month. A family could blow their entire retirement nest egg with one of these events. Now you have left the surviving spouse in a less than ideal retirement situation.

Another pothole is drinking the Kool-Aid of conventional wisdom to delay, defer, and deduct.

If you have $3 million in an IRA, that's a pretty good amount for retirement, but here's the problem: no taxes have been paid yet. And to get that converted incrementally is painful. But that pain pales in comparison to the pain you'd feel having to pay future tax rates of 40%, 50%, or even 60%, like they have in Europe, in the years ahead.

The third pothole is the assumption that what has worked in the past will continue to work the same way in the future.

To provide you with a nonhypothetical example, let me tell you about a recent experience. We recently had a couple that just joined our firm as new clients. They'd been working with Vanguard for years, and their money was invested in the S&P 500 and a technology index because of its low cost. After they lost 25% in 2022, they were looking at their accounts and recognizing that they needed to do something different.

That realization didn't happen until the markets started spiraling downward.

We're seeing people coming out of the woodwork, realizing that they have to do something different. They thought everything was OK, without considering how 40-year-high inflation rates or spiking interest rates have changed the game.

The dips and slides in the market have reinforced the need to take a proactive approach to investing. They realize that everyone needs a real financial plan with true retirement planning and an annual tax plan to prepare for the road ahead.

CHAPTER 14

IT'S NOT AN EVENT, IT'S A PROCESS

Moving to Tax-Free Involves Years of Planning and Strategic Intent

"The most difficult thing is the decision to act, the rest is merely tenacity. The fears are paper tigers. You can do anything you decide to do. You can act to change and control your life; and the procedure, the process is its own reward."

—AMELIA EARHART[75]

Moving to tax-free is not an event; it is a process that involves years of planning and strategic intent.

Unfortunately, in the tax preparation industry, clients have been allowed to drive the narrative by asking how much they're going to have to pay in taxes *this year*. Everything is so shortsighted and right in front of our faces.

The response from the accounting and the tax community has

---

75 "Quotes," The Official Licensing Website of Amelia Earhart, accessed May 1, 2023, https://www.ameliaearhart.com/quotes/.https://www.ameliaearhart.com/quotes/.

been to placate and encourage that sentiment. Everybody is looking for a magic pill that they can use as a one-time fix.

And then, next year, they're focused again on getting that same short-term fix, without a second thought for the long-term ramifications.

Harvesting Your Crops

As I said in Chapter 3, moving to tax-free is a lot like farming. You cannot plant seeds one day, then harvest your crops the next—you have to water them, weed them, feed them, drain the field, fight off pests, and be out there every day working in the orchard and watching it, so the pests don't destroy your crop.

After all that work comes the harvest.

The move to tax-free is similar. It takes time and effort and good planning. And because the starting and ending points are so far apart, it requires steady, incremental progress.

By the time you get done, all that forward progress can make a dramatic difference in your life.

If you start on this process in your fifties and sixties and you work on it for 10 or 12 or 15 years, and then you retire at 65 or 70, it can set you up for financial stability for the next 20 or 30 years with a **0%** tax bracket, or as close to zero as possible.

The Impact of Software

The right financial planning software can make a dramatic difference in your quest to move to tax-free.

Most financial planning software uses a Monte Carlo simulation for statistical analysis. The computer will make 1,000 iterations—high, low, and everything in between—of possible rates of return on your portfolio over a period of, say, 30 years, and it will statistically prognosticate the probability of a client or couple in retirement running out of money.[76]

A lot of financial planning software will use this type of analysis to project what's ahead.

Financial planning manually—with inflation rates constantly shifting, and tax rates bound to change, and investments with floors and hedges, and market exposure, and so many other variables—is all but impossible to accurately project the future.

Software can help you illustrate and track your marginal—and, more importantly, your effective—tax rate. Software will illustrate your risk tolerance with conservative and aggressive investment strategies.

If you rely on safe investments, depending on your situation, you may not have enough growth in your portfolio to sustain your standard of living against higher inflation rates. So, software can give us the ability to coach clients and have them arrive at a place where

---

76 Will Kenton, "Monte Carlo Simulation: History, How It Works, and 4 Key Steps," Investopedia, last updated March 26, 2023, https://www.investopedia.com/terms/m/montecarlosimulation.asp.

they can sleep at night but still know that their portfolio is going to potentially grow in the face of inflation and rising taxes.

Income Streams

The value of strategic tax planning becomes increasingly clear when considering your buckets of taxable, tax-deferred, tax-exempt, and tax-free money.

Think of each of those buckets not just each year for tax return purposes but in the years ahead, since the money from those buckets will be used at different times and in different amounts to weave together the best tax scenario for you each year.

If you need $100,000 from your investment portfolio in year three, for example, you could prepare for that by investing today in a bond fund that's paying a return of 4%—meaning $12,000 growth during that time.

Years 6 to 10, you can be a little more aggressive because you don't have to touch that money right away. You can get a higher rate of return by being willing to tie up your money for a longer period of time. These time frames represent income ladders, the income that we have locked in for these specific increments.

The rule of 72 tells us mathematically (approximately) how long it will take to double our money.[77]

With the rule of 72, if you divide 72 by your interest rate, it will

---

77 Will Kenton, "The Rule of 72: Definition, Usefulness, and How to Use It," Investopedia, last updated March 9, 2023, https://www.investopedia.com/terms/r/ruleof72.asp.

THE 4 TYPES OF TAX TREATMENTS OF YOUR INVESTMENTS

REPOSITION TO TAX-FREE

TAXABLE

- Dividends
- Interest
- Capital Gains
- Rental Income

TAX-DEFERRED

- IRAs
- 401ks
- Retirement Plans
- Annuities

TAX-EXEMPT

- Municipal Bond Interest
- *Is included in "Provisions Income"*
- *Increases taxability of social security*

"TAX FREE" TAX-EXEMPT

- Roth IRAs
- Life Insurance *(LIRP: Life Insurance Retirement Plan)*

tell you the number of years you need to double your money. As you spend down your money in your fixed income accounts, you can let your money build in your longer-term growth accounts, and then you can take the growth and flop it back over into your income account, re-create your income ladder, and leave your seed money in your growth buckets to grow and double again.

Essentially, what you're doing with this type of planning is creating a perpetual income stream that you can never outlive.

A Pile of Baloney

A big misconception is that people are going to live on less income in retirement.

That is the biggest pile of baloney I've ever heard.

When my clients retire, they want to travel and play golf and join a club. They want to spend time with their friends and family and go on big trips every year or two. They've been sacrificing and scrimping to put their children through college, and now that they have an empty nest, it's their time to live.

What I have observed is that during retirement, people need about the same amount of income or even more income than they had during their working years.

And those who've saved diligently and worked hard to implement tax-free strategies potentially enjoy an even higher standard of after-tax income in retirement.

Lots of people rely on Social Security and Medicare in retirement, but those programs are underfunded right now, and we are headed for a fiscal storm in the United States.

Many people are worried that these programs will go away at some point in the future. These programs likely will not go away totally. They are very likely going to pay you less than what you are expecting or will need. We are already seeing evidence of this with additional Medicare (IRMAA, income-related monthly adjustment amounts) premiums and penalties if your income goes over $194,000 if you are MFJ (married filing jointly).[78]

Pay a little bit now, or pay a lot later.

If you are diligent now about moving to tax-free—instead of waiting and staying with it until you're close to or entering retirement—you won't have to make such big Roth conversions later, and you may be able to get to the point where some or all of your Social Security isn't taxable at all.

Consider an imaginary couple, David and Sally, who have $3 million in their retirement accounts.

They need help moving their tax-deferred money out of their 401(k)s and traditional IRAs into Roth IRAs and moving their taxable investments from traditional taxable accounts into tax-free life insurance retirement plans. They're working toward getting to a point in the next four or five years where they could be enjoying $200,000 a year in tax-free income with zero taxes. Social Security benefits make up $40,000 of that $200,000 total. Those Social Security benefits will be income tax–free as well. Imagine that $200,000

---

78 "2022 Medicare Part B Premium Costs & IRMAA," Harvard, accessed May 1, 2023, https://hr.harvard.edu/files/humanresources/files/medicare_irmaa.pdf.

annually in retirement income including your Social Security bene-fits, and all of it income tax–free.

Yes, that's truly tax-free.

People may look at that and think, *That's unfair and unjust that the rich are cheating the system.* And that's simply not the case. People who choose to pursue this path have paid their taxes up front, and now they won't have to pay them in retirement because they've moved their money into tax-free vehicles.

These opportunities are available to everyone. Taking advantage of the U.S. tax laws that are available to you is up to you. If you are willing to pay the price of delayed gratification and to be intentional about moving to tax-free vehicles that can benefit from the tax system that our government has provided to us, then you, too, can use the tax laws to protect your family from future higher tax rates in the United States.

For example, let's take someone who's 50 years old who put away $30,000 in a Roth 401(k). Let's assume that they are in the 20% effective tax rate and an additional 5% is taken out for state taxes, so 25% all in.

That would require them to pay $7,500 in taxes this year on their Roth 401(k) contribution.

Who would willingly volunteer to pay that amount in taxes if they didn't have to?

You would, if you are consciously trying to move your money to tax-free investment vehicles.

That's the price you have to pay if you want your money to escape the worldwide gravitational pull of the U.S. tax system. If you want future tax-free income for your life, your spouse's life, and at least 10 years of your children's lives after you die, then moving to tax-free is the road you have to take.

Three Key Needs in Retirement Planning

Moving to tax-free is not a DIY process.

There are a lot of professionals who claim to be able to help you plan for your retirement, and in the next chapter, we present questions that you can ask your professionals to see if they are adept, qualified, competent, and capable of helping you achieve your move to tax-free.

The core of your retirement planning should involve these advisors:

- An astute wealth manager / financial planner / CFP® professional or CPWA®
- A sharp tax professional (EA—enrolled agent—or CPA)
- A competent estate planning attorney

All these professionals should be willing to work together collaboratively for your benefit.

Your move to tax-free is a gestalt shift, a focus on the bigger picture and how the pieces all fit together, and your advisors—while helpful in specific areas—may not individually have expertise in every area you need.

Your Dream Team of Advisors

Simply put, you need a true wealth manager / financial planner.

A wealth manager, even if they aren't preparing your taxes, will help you in your tax-planning efforts. Lots of people view wealth managers and financial planners as interchangeable, but financial planners may not do investment management or tax planning.

A CPA or EA tax professional—is obviously crucial for your tax planning—likely won't know about your investments and likely will not have been involved in how you structure the investments in your portfolios.

And with estate planning attorneys, once they draw up documents, you may not see them again for 5 to 10 years.

Dream Team Priorities

Your first priority should be to make sure that you have all of your financial planning instruments and documents structured in the right way.

Some of these include a retirement income plan that is up to date and maintained in financial planning software that synchronizes with your investment accounts to keep your net worth current.

This financial planning software becomes your compass to tell you (through all the various ups and downs of the markets and changes in tax law) if you're going to be OK through your full retirement.

Second, you're going to want to have a tax professional who has tax-planning software. They will assist you every year by putting together a tax plan. This tax plan should create options for plan A, plan B, and plan C. Look at the choices you have available to you in implementing your move to tax-free.

Third, you will want to work with an investment professional who is experienced and competent as an IRA expert. They should be able to provide you with all the IRA beneficiary planning techniques required by the passage of the SECURE Act and, as of 2022, SECURE Act 2.0.

Your beneficiaries will have to pull the proceeds out of your IRA and Roth IRA within just 10 years after you die. There are many advanced strategies that could be beneficial for your family, including an IRA beneficiary trust.

You will want an IRA expert who is familiar with using advanced IRA beneficiary designations, including sole primary beneficiary, contingent beneficiary, and tertiary beneficiary designations if they make sense with your planning objectives.

This level of planning will give your beneficiaries choices and options, flexibility that they can achieve no other way.

It is likely you will want to split your IRA into several different IRA accounts in order to take advantage of some of the most advanced IRA planning techniques available to you for your beneficiaries.

If your IRA investment professional is not providing planning at this level, you are most likely going to want to find someone who can competently advise you in structuring your IRA and Roth IRA accounts.

Fourth, much of the most important implementation in this area of planning will be completed after your death. Assuming you have put the proper planning in place, your spouse and your beneficiaries can benefit from that planning.

However, with success and financial wherewithal comes the responsibility of stewardship.

Your spouse and beneficiaries will likely have to deal with the complexity of moving parts, tax strategy implementation, and trust administration.

Protecting your move to tax-free without blowing up all the planning that you've put in place will require sage advice. You'll need to be able to evaluate your tax professional and make sure they're right for you.

Non-Correlated Tax-Free Investment Vehicles

In 2022, Americans experienced both a 19.44% decline in the equity markets represented by the S&P 500 and a 13.06% decline in the intermediate bond markets such as the AGG (the Bloomberg Aggregate bond index).[79]

This correlation of the equity and fixed income markets losing value in a parallel fashion only takes place approximately 10% of the time, according to some analysts. Think back to the analogy of

---

79 Howard Silverblatt, "U.S. Equities Market Attributes December 2022," S&P Dow Jones Indices, https://www.spglobal.com/spdji/en/commentary/article/us-equities-market-attributes-december-2022.

two roller coasters running side by side, going up and down at the same time. That is exactly what you don't want to have happen to your retirement accounts when you're retired. If all your asset classes are correlated, and they go down simultaneously and you're drawing money out for your retirement needs at the same time, your portfolio may never recover.

Investments that are correlated can expose you to "sequence of return risk," which is acknowledged by many retirement professionals as the number one risk to a retiree's successful retirement. If the sequence is wrong, and you lose too much money too early in retirement, your portfolio may never recover and provide you with the income that you seek through your full life expectancy.

I would like to introduce you to two non-correlated tax-free investment vehicles. That's a mouthful, so let me break that down. "Non-correlated" means that they do not correlate to the movement of either the stock or the bond markets. And because these markets can sometimes move in opposite directions, that means that it doesn't move in any direction, really. This provides a stable value, and that's what many people seek in retirement: stable value.

So how do we provide stable value with these volatility buffers? In my opinion, the only way they can provide this non-correlation protection is if they do not lose value when either the bond or stock markets drop in. The value that these tools provide is protection in the face of volatility.

The Life Insurance Retirement Plan (LIRP) Funded by a Cash Value: Indexed Universal Life Insurance Policy

How can a life insurance policy provide you with a non-correlated income stream? Using a cash-value indexed universal life insurance policy to provide tax-free retirement income may provide protections against losing principal.

That means that if the stock market goes down, your account may be guaranteed against losing any value. Similarly, if the bond markets go down, you can be guaranteed against losing any value in your policy.

Now, why are these features so very important? Because if you are taking income from your stock portfolio and the stock market loses 20%, you should immediately stop drawing down from those accounts and switch over to your life insurance retirement plan (LIRP) to receive your income needs.

When you take income from your LIRP, those proceeds are received in the form of a loan against the policy. Because the loan is made from the general account of the insurance company, your money is left invested in the investments that you have selected. And even though those investments are guaranteed against loss of principal, you are not drawing down value from your account. You're just borrowing money from the insurance company, which collateralizes it with your cash value from your life insurance policy.

When the stock or bond markets recover and go higher, you can sell your gains in those portfolios and repay the loan against your life insurance policy. By managing your portfolio with non-correlated assets that are tax-free, you can provide more stability of income, avoid selling at a loss when the markets (stock, bond, and real estate) are down, and generate tax-free income in retirement without cutting back on your spendable income needs.

Using this "buckets of money" approach to diversifying your investments among non-correlated tax-free invest vehicles can improve the statistical probability of your retirement plan successfully providing income through your full life expectancy.

CHAPTER 15

QUESTIONS TO CONSIDER

Use These Questions to Help Find the Right Professional to Help You Make Your Move to Tax-Free

"The man who asks a question is a fool for a minute, the man who does not ask is a fool for life."

—PROVERB OFTEN ATTRIBUTED TO CONFUCIUS

It's time to evaluate your tax professional and other experts.

Is your current tax professional the right professional to help you make your move to tax-free?

If you aren't familiar with tax-free strategies, it can be daunting to know what to say when speaking to your tax professional. To make this easier for you, I've listed some key questions below that should help you sort out top-shelf proactive tax professionals from tax historians who are still looking backward and just reporting what has happened to you tax-wise in the past year. Plain tax preparers are... not what you want.

We want you to look for tax and financial professionals who are regularly preparing forward-looking tax projections for their clients. Many tax professionals aren't comfortable with, or familiar with, annual tax-planning and tax-free strategies. Why, you ask? Because they are so busy preparing last year's tax returns for their other tax clients that they don't have the time, capacity, experience, or expertise on their teams to perform this type of forward-looking tax-planning work.

These questions can help you evaluate the tax-planning preparedness of your current tax expert. If you don't have an ideal tax-planning expert, these questions may help you in evaluating and interviewing your new tax-planning professional.

Questions for a Tax Professional

1. Is there a Roth IRA or Roth 401(k) option available in your own retirement plan?

If a CPA or tax preparer does not use Roth IRAs or Roth 401(k)s—with their clients or for themselves—they may not be able to help you pursue a tax-free retirement. It is so surprising to me how many professionals, including CPAs, EAs, other tax professionals, and estate planning attorneys, don't personally use and recommend tax-free Roth IRAs and Roth 401(k) retirement accounts.

2. What percentage of your clients are you preparing an annual tax plan for each year?

In our industry, tax professionals make their money by preparing taxes. When they are preparing your taxes, they are looking backward—they are reporting what transpired in your life over the last year. They are not helping you look forward and project what strategic action you could take to lower your taxes in the future.

If your tax professional is not doing a lot of tax planning as a regular part of their business, then you're likely not getting the type of tax advice that you need to start moving to tax-free.

Practice makes perfect in any profession. If your tax professional only prepares a forward-looking tax plan for a select few clients, they are not going to have a breadth and depth of tax-planning experience and knowledge to provide you with the level of tax-planning advice that you seek in order to make the move to tax-free (or at least begin to make the move to tax-free).

3. Are you familiar with life insurance retirement plans (LIRPs)?

    a. If yes, do you have one yourself?

    b. Do you have any clients who have them?

    c. Have you recommended one to a client?

Experts should be providing guidance with their clients' best interest in mind. But there are a lot of professionals who have the misguided opinion that life insurance is bad and expensive and not worthwhile. They tell their clients to buy term life insurance—*buy term and invest the difference.* This is all well and good, but the difference you invest is now in a taxable or tax-deferred account that doesn't get all the benefits of tax-free growth that permanent cash-value life can provide in an indexed universal life (IUL) policy.

Life insurance retirement plans (LIRPs) have matured and come into their own in the last five years. And this industry, the tax industry, is made up of lots of gray hairs who've been in the business 20, 30, 40 years. A lot of times, they can work part of the year doing tax preparation and take the rest of the year off. It's a great part-time job.

As a result, they've grown old in the industry and have long ago formed their opinions, and there may be a bias around life insurance. Not enough tax pros have bothered to educate themselves. So when someone brings up life insurance, they've already formed their opinion about it. *Oh, that's a bad investment,* they'll say. It's important for tax professionals to be knowledgeable and competent when it comes to all the cutting-edge tax-planning vehicles that are available.

4. Looking forward, what do you think my future tax rates are going to do—stay the same, go lower, or go higher?

This question helps you test your tax professional's ability to map out the path ahead. CPAs and many tax professionals are very risk averse in general. This isn't necessarily a bad thing! Tax professionals typically look backward and report what has happened—we're not often helping clients plan to look forward.

On the other hand, financial planners try to look forward, but they aren't qualified to do so when it comes to taxes, since they aren't true tax professionals. And then many investment managers and money managers act in a charade as if they're financial planners, but many don't have the training or qualifications to truly create, implement, and manage financial plans.

You want a tax professional who can look forward and backward, someone who can blend the caution of a CPA and the vision of a forward-looking qualified financial planner. Asking this question will help you recognize if a tax professional is wearing those multiple hats and if they are being productive in looking into the future. They should be able to recognize major trends on the horizon—because otherwise, you will likely be missing opportunities over the long haul.

5. Do you prepare Social Security projection calculations for your clients? If so, how many have you prepared in the last year?

Some financial advisors are set up to provide these types of calculations, but CPAs typically don't. A good tax professional will be adept at doing these calculations. Preparing just a few of these calculations annually is not likely the answer you're seeking.

6. I want to plan to pay less taxes over my remaining life. What are your recommendations for how I plan to do that?

If you are really focused on moving to tax-free and not just getting a yearly tax deduction, a tax professional will have answers—and questions—in response to this inquiry.

They should be able to provide you with robust long-term ideas like what I have provided to you in this book.

Questions for a Financial Advisor or Wealth Manager

In a similar vein, I wanted to leave you with potential questions to ask a financial advisor to see if they are the right fit for you as you pursue a tax-free retirement. The answers to these questions should help you recognize if they are committed to these strategies—and if they practice what they preach and are really devoted to this type of work or are just dipping their toe in the water.

- Do you have Roth IRA or Roth 401(k) options available in your practice?
- What percentage of your clients do you help convert to Roth IRAs or encourage to fund their Roth 401(k)s?
- Do you own a Roth IRA yourself?
    - » If so, how big is it compared to your other investment accounts?
- Are you preparing annual tax plans for your clients?
    - » For what percentage of your clients do you prepare an annual tax plan?
- Are you licensed for life insurance?
- Do you advise clients about life insurance retirement plans (LIRPs)?
- Do you have a LIRP yourself?
    - » How much do you fund into that every year?
- What other tax-free strategies do you use?
- Do you use and recommend:
    - » 1031/721 like-kind exchanges?
    - » Revocable living trusts in community property states?

> » HSAs?
>
> » 529 plans?
>
> » Qualified charitable distributions (QCDs)?
>
> » Cash balance or defined benefit plans with 401(h) options?

- What percentage of your clients are in the process of converting their IRAs to Roth IRAs on an annual basis?
- What study groups do you belong to, or what training do you take annually to keep your edge as a tax planning professional?

Questions for an Estate Planning Attorney

1. Do you work on a flat fee or an hourly basis?

In my experience, those who work on an hourly basis game the system, whereas those who work on a flat, fixed fee will have a list of specific deliverables. I have found these specialists (law firms that specialize in estate planning and work on a flat fee basis) to be the best at their craft.

2. When you prepare an estate planning package for a couple, which documents are included in your flat fee program?

Make sure they include the following documents:

- A revocable living trust
- Wills or pour-over wills
- A durable financial power of attorney

- A durable health care power of attorney
- A living will
- A mental health care power of attorney
- A real estate beneficiary deed, if needed

3. If you prepare estate planning documents for clients, do you fund the trust specifically for real estate and other nonliquid assets as an included service?

One of the biggest problems we see is that clients will get the trust document, put it on the shelf, and never fund it. If the trust doesn't own anything, it doesn't control anything—you have to move the title of all the assets that you want in the trust into the trust to fund the trust.

4. If I want to leave some money to charity, how would you advise me to include that in my documents?

This is one of the most common wealth transfer tax-planning disasters I run into involving estate planning. Clients will engage an estate planning attorney, and they will specifically want to leave a chunk of money to a church, college, or medical school that they attended. Let's say they want to leave a quarter of a million, $250,000, to their desired charity.

When they see the estate planning attorney, they'll say, "Hey, I want to leave $250,000 to my alma mater," and the attorney goes, "OK, fine." And the attorney will draw up the trust that way, leaving

$250,000 of the client's taxable investments as a gift to the university upon the death of the client.

The client may have a total estate of around $8 million: $3 million in IRA funds, another $3 million in regular taxable money, and a home worth $2 million. They have two children as well.

They have the goal to leave the majority of their money to their children, but they're charitably inclined as well, and want to leave the $250,000 to the medical school.

What often happens in these circumstances is that the attorneys are really good at drawing up the documents, but they're not so good at the tax-planning side of things. I always tell clients, "Most estate planning attorneys require some tax supervision because they are used to controlling everything through their trust document."

Many of them will take the steps that are the easiest for them to control with the trust document, but this may not necessarily be what is in the best interest of the family when you consider the tax consequences.

When the taxpayer dies, their taxable investments will receive a step-up in basis. That is the cost basis of the taxable investments, be they stock or real estate, which can receive a step-up in basis from the cost to the current fair market value as of the deceased's date of death. (Assuming the assets are titled correctly in trust and as community property in a community property state.)

Let's say the $3 million the client holds in the stock market has a cost basis of $1,500,000.

If the client leaves the legacy gift of $250,000 out of that taxable account, then the attorney just caused the family to miss out on $250,000 of tax-free assets.

If instead the client is correctly advised and leaves the taxable funds to the children, the children would receive a full step-up in basis and would pay zero taxes on those funds.

The alma mater, because it's a charity, doesn't pay income taxes. But what happens in this scenario is the kids get beat out of the taxes on $250,000 at ordinary income tax rates (IRA funds) that would've come to them income tax–free.

This disaster could be avoided if instead the client separates out a second IRA account and transfers $250,000 into that IRA with the charitable organization named as the contingent beneficiary. The client can leave the special IRA account to the medical school. He can name his wife as the primary beneficiary and the university as the contingent beneficiary. If he dies and his wife still has enough money in other investments, she can disclaim the separate $250,000 IRA account, and the money will then go directly to the university. The doctor and his wife and their children will not pay any taxes, and the university will not pay any taxes, because they are a nonprofit. The only ones that get beat out of any money with this tax-free plan are the IRS and state governments.

On the other hand, if the attorney plans the gift with taxable funds controlled through the trust, the family will have to recognize and pay ordinary income taxes on all of the $250,000 left in the IRA account.

The worst thing about this is that you can't fix it on the back end. If they don't set it up charitably from the IRA on the front end, if the university is not set up as the contingent beneficiary behind the wife, there's no way to fix it. He dies. It's over. Done, checkmate, they lose. They pay taxes they didn't need to.

5. What assets do you recommend that I move and title into my trust?

You want to listen and see what the attorney is going to say. Obviously, the primary residence, a secondary residence, the lake cabin, and any rental properties that may be held in an LLC could and should most likely be titled into the trust.

For example, you can't take an IRA and title that into your trust because it creates a taxable event as soon as you distribute the funds from the IRA account.

Some attorneys might send instructions to the IRA custodian and suggest naming the trust as the beneficiary, but there are very important reasons why you generally don't want to do that. First, if a couple is married, we want to name the spouse as sole primary beneficiary because, as an EDB, or "eligible designated beneficiary," they get the benefits of being able to stretch that IRA out over their remaining life or transfer it into their own name. (Notice that I did not say "roll it over into her own name.")

So you never want to name the trust as the beneficiary in those cases.

You generally don't want to name nonqualified annuities in the name of the trust either. If you title a nonqualified annuity between a husband and wife in joint ownership, and one of them dies, as soon as they pass away, if the annuity is titled in the trust, it immediately has to pay out the death benefit, and if it's nonqualified, guess what? The surviving spouse has to recognize all of the growth in that account and pay all the taxes at ordinary income tax rates, all in that tax year.

If it's owned jointly, the surviving spouse gets to continue the contract, tax-deferred, and won't have to recognize the income and pay the taxes if they continue the contract.

I often see attorneys wanting to move the annuities into the trust. But the annuities are already self-completing—they already have a death beneficiary designation. You don't need to move them into the trust. For couples, it is generally best to title nonqualified annuities in joint ownership.

6. Does the attorney expect the clients to re-title the life insurance policy in the trust?

Unfortunately, I find some attorneys who want to re-title the life insurance into the trust without a valid reason. Some want to title the life insurance in trust for a reason. And they tend to do this on purpose. Life insurance policies have beneficiaries. You can name a primary, a contingent, and a tertiary beneficiary. And I'm OK naming the trust as the tertiary beneficiary—but usually, I want a spouse as the primary beneficiary, and then I want the kids as the contingent beneficiaries because the death benefits are income tax–free, and you don't have to involve trust administration or a trustee in the claiming process. This is very easy.

It doesn't have to get complicated. The goal is to provide the least amount of hassle for the survivors.

If the life insurance policy is re-titled into the trust and the trust is the beneficiary, now it becomes part of the trust estate, and the trust needs to be administered. Everything is paid out based on the instructions of the trust.

Attorneys often charge 1% of the trust assets to administer the trust.

So, if you've got a $1 million death benefit when a parent dies, if the life insurance is titled into the trust, now it's an asset of the trust—meaning now the attorneys are going to charge $10,000 to administer the claiming of the life insurance death benefits, when you could have just left that money to the grieving relatives.

There are a couple of rare instances where it may make sense to title the life insurance policy in the trust, such as when the client has a big taxable estate. But much of the time, you just want to name individual people and leave the money to the relatives.

7. How do many estate planning attorneys approach charitable giving?

The financial advisor really has to be the one to help clients with the planning on charitable giving. Attorneys are helpful for document-preparation purposes, but in the planning of whether you're going to use a donor-advised fund, a family foundation, or a charitable remainder trust, the financial advisor needs to be involved as well.

Many attorneys don't care or worry about the tax bill coming due for a family. They're trying to achieve the client's wishes the easiest way they can, using their estate planning documents. They are not necessarily considering all the tax ramifications. So, in their minds, if they hear that the client wants to leave money to charity, they write it into the trust, and they're done with it. They've addressed it.

The thing about estate planning attorneys is that, once you meet with them and get everything sorted, you might not see them again for 5 to 10 years, whereas my clients typically see our team two to four times a year. They have regular contact with us, and we work with them on their investments, financial planning, taxes, tax planning, and moving to tax-free.

A Heavy Lift

For tax professionals, learning the skills to help clients move to tax-free is a heavy lift.

It's a heavy lift because they've grown their tax practices, and they're so busy with annual tax return preparation that the vast majority of them don't have the time, or bandwidth capacity, to provide long-term tax planning.

The only way a professional can really do this work is to hire somebody—either someone whose only job is tax planning or someone who can relieve them of their day-to-day duties so they can worry about tax planning.

Clients typically aren't used to paying for tax planning. They're used to paying for tax preparation. So, it's a different sale for the tax professional.

A Difficult Bridge to Cross

Accountants, by their very nature, are typically more conservative and reserved—they're usually not your gregarious, outspoken salesperson types.

It's hard for them to ask for more money and to charge appropriately for tax planning.

Their very nature is not to sell more billable hours or more projects for tax planning to clients. Even if the clients realize the benefits and the accountant can explain the benefits to the clients, the clients have to be willing to pay extra for the tax planning. That can sometimes be a difficult bridge for tax professionals to cross.

The Cost of Business

We do tax planning as part of our overall wealth management services.

We have enough people—including CPAs and EAs—on staff that we have the capacity to do tax planning all year.

What normally happens is that CPAs and tax professionals who are only doing tax prep during tax season might only be busy from January through April 15, and then on to extensions.

And the firm has to have enough people and capacity to do tax planning year-round, not just during tax season.

Before you get revenue from doing tax planning, you've got to spend money on salaries to pay the people who are working on tax planning—to grow, you have to spend money.

It's a huge investment in wages for the firm.

But if you're committed to this work, and you see an opportunity, you have to be willing to make that investment in the firm, to employ the people who can do the work, and to be willing to ask for the tax-planning fee.

I Walk My Talk

When I seek advice, I want it from a professional who has already performed this work for others many times and has successfully produced the work for themselves as well. I think you should hold your professional advisors to the same standard.

As a professional, I have a very large life insurance retirement plan. I contribute $75,000 each year to my plan with after-tax investments.

My wife and I both contribute the maximum amount allowed every year ($30,000 each) to our Roth 401(k) accounts. I have also converted the right amount of my IRA to a Roth IRA. I own the real estate for both of our business offices, and our wealth management firm rents the office building from me.

I walk my talk. I know what I am talking about because I have experienced what I am sharing with you firsthand, both on behalf of myself personally and on behalf of my clients whom I have served for more than 27 years. I have been blessed with and enjoyed great financial success myself. I am humbled by this work. I work with clients who are far more financially successful than I am, so I am well qualified to talk to you about your financial success. I discuss these tax-free tactics with my clients and prospects on a very direct and personal basis.

Do you really want to use tax, legal, and financial professionals who have less investment experience than you do?

How about trying to set up a life insurance retirement plan with an advisor who has never set one up for themselves? They don't have their own plan to show you what they are doing to move to tax-free.

A lot of people question the importance of a good long-term care insurance policy. I have a long-term care policy and show clients my plan and how it compares to traditional long-term care insurance plans.

I share all of this with you to let you know that I walk my talk. I am the real deal. I know what I am talking about because I practice these concepts every day and have lived them for years.

I hope my sharing helps to instill confidence in you, helping you decide that you, too, can do this. That it is well worth your time, energy, and effort to take this path to a tax-free retirement. You, too, can take the steps necessary to begin moving to tax-free. I promise.

Because if I can do it, then you, too, can do it.

CHAPTER 16

ESTATE PLANNING AND TAX-FREE WEALTH TRANSFER

Leave Your Beneficiaries Tax-Free Assets Instead of a Tax Bill—and Headaches

"If you do not have a will or plan for your estate, then the government has one for you."

—SHEZ CHRISTOPHER

I have another Boy Scout story for you, this one from when I served as the Boy Scout leader for the 11-year-old Scouts. We planned a Scout campout one weekend over near Sedona, up above Oak Creek Canyon in the tall pines. We had taught the boys how to prepare tinfoil dinners, and this was their chance to prepare them themselves and cook them over an open fire.

After a two-hour ride in the trucks, we arrived at our camping spot right about dark. The Arizona summer monsoons had come in and rained really hard before we arrived at our camping spot, and everything was soaking wet, but we let the boys know that they could build a fire with wet wood if they could get it started and burning hot enough. The boys struggled at first, but eventually they got their fires started. Even so, they had a hard time getting the fires big enough to create the hot coals needed to cook their tinfoil dinners.

My son Nick and the Scout paired with him, Brennan, had an especially tough time. It was dark and cold, and Brennan had forgotten to bring his flashlight, so they had to share Nick's flashlight. Brennan finally got his tinfoil dinner on the hot coals, and after five minutes passed, he asked me, "Is it done yet?"

"No," I told him, "you need to let it cook for about twenty-five to thirty minutes at least."

Over the next half hour, Brennan asked me every three to five minutes if he could take his tinfoil dinner off the fire. Finally, he could not wait any longer, and without Nick's flashlight, he pulled his tinfoil dinner from the fire and opened it up with his pocketknife. "Brother Hosler, you made me cook it too long! The chicken is all crumbly and dried out!" he yelled. He was really upset.

I took my flashlight and went over to help him. Together, we looked at the food more closely.

"Brennan, this does not look like chicken, it looks like chocolate chip cookies," I told him. "Look in your backpack and see if your tinfoil dinner is in there."

Sure enough, it was—his mother had made his tinfoil dinner for him, and she had also packed chocolate chip cookies in tinfoil. He had not known what was in his backpack, what was dinner, and what was dessert. Poor Brennan…his tinfoil dinner was raw and uncooked, his fire had died out, and there were not enough hot coals to cook his dinner. And his chocolate chip cookies were burned too.

He had not properly prepared for the campout, and he suffered the consequences of his lack of preparation. I ended up sharing my dinner with him.

With estate planning, being prepared and taking the right steps is the difference between being ready to help others and having to go without or requiring a hand.

Being prepared and getting your affairs in order is crucial to making sure that your money and belongings are passed down as you intend. The way you structure and title your assets will be the difference between leaving your beneficiaries tax-free assets and potentially leaving them a tax bill—along with headaches.

Titling

Titling refers to the *who* and *how* of owning or taking title to your assets. Your assets can be titled or owned by you individually, jointly with a spouse or other person, or in a trust. A trust may hold assets on your behalf for the benefit of the beneficiaries of the trust. Usually, the beneficiaries will be you and your spouse, your children, or other heirs.

The Right Team in Place

Your estate planning team should include your:

- Tax-planning accountant

- Financial planner
- Investment or wealth manager
- Estate planning attorney

All these professionals should work collaboratively to help you move toward your goal. They should all understand the assets you own and how they're titled. They should all know how you want to handle your beneficiary designations on the various accounts that use beneficiary designations.

Those beneficiary designations are especially important for assets like IRAs and 401(k)s, which cannot be held as joint accounts—they are by their very definition individual retirement accounts. Instead, a spouse can be named as a sole primary beneficiary. You can also name contingent and tertiary beneficiaries. You might be wondering why you should name a tertiary beneficiary. Let's say the husband is the owner of a traditional IRA. He has named his wife his sole primary beneficiary. Their children might be named contingent beneficiaries, and the grandchildren might be named tertiary beneficiaries.

Babies are born into the family, people die, and you may have extended relatives you wish to leave your money to. Having the correct beneficiary designations in place will help you avoid getting your money tied up in the courts when you die.

Getting Up to Speed

When people engage our firm to help them with their estate planning, they tend to fall into a couple of camps in terms of titling their assets and estate planning.

1. Some of them have not done anything yet. These tend to be younger people.

2. Some have done some things—maybe they have a will or a trust—but inevitably, most of the time, what they have is out of date. When they come to work with us, they come knowing that they're not on top of everything and need some help.

Don't worry. According to CNBC, a new survey by senior living referral service Caring.com reports that 67% of Americans don't have any estate planning in place.[80]

People are typically aware of the importance of reviewing their beneficiary designations and keeping their legal documents up to date, and they realize they need help in bringing them current and keeping them current. Maybe there are changes in their families: A new grandchild. A death. A divorce. Or the tax laws have changed, and their legal documents need to be updated.

A lot of people are like deer in the headlights at the onset. We review their beneficiary designations every year, and if a client has issues with their trust, we discuss them. We encourage each client to have their attorney update their (medical and financial) powers of attorney every three to five years. Banks may consider powers of attorney that are more than two to three years old as "stale" and have been known not to honor those older financial powers of attorney.

---

80   Lorie Konish, "67% of Americans Have No Estate Plan, Survey Finds. Here's How to Get Started on One," CNBC, April 11, 2022, https://www.cnbc.com/2022/04/11/67percent-of-americans-have-no-estate-plan-heres-how-to-get-started-on-one.html.

Community Property States

Even something as basic as refinancing a home mortgage can cause problems with asset titling if you aren't careful.

With the low interest rates in recent years, people were refinancing their homes into lower-interest-rate loans. If you hold title to your house in a trust, the bank will have you take the house out of the trust and place it in your own name in order to refinance the property.

Once the refinance is complete, you are supposed to re-title the house back into the revocable trust. But there is nobody there to hold your hand and make sure you take these important steps.

That wrinkle can be especially concerning for residents in community property states, of which there are nine—Arizona, California, Idaho, Louisiana, Nevada, New Mexico, Texas, Washington, and Wisconsin.

In those states, property and assets that are properly titled as "community property with rights of survivorship" can receive all the benefits that the tax laws provide to a surviving spouse in a community property state.[81]

Consider this example. Let's say a married couple in a community property state doesn't re-title the house back into their living trust after a refinance where the bank made them take it out of their revocable living trust and move it into their own names (joint tenants) for the refinance. If one of the spouses dies without the house being

---

81   "Community Property States vs. Common Law," Asset Protection Planners, accessed May 1, 2023, https://www.assetprotectionplanners.com/planning/community-property-states/.

transferred back into the trust where it is held in community property with rights of survivorship, here are the consequences.

They bought the house for $250,000, and it's now worth $1.2 million.

If the surviving spouse needs or wants to sell the house, let's consider the tax implications. The cost basis on the home would be $300,000 (the purchase price and the $50,000 in home improvements). The surviving spouse would get to claim one half of the cost basis, so her cost basis would be $150,000. She also gets a step-up in basis on one half of the fair market value (FMV), which is usually the sales price. In this case, that would be $600,000, assuming a date of death value of $1,200,000.

Let's assume a sale price of $1,200,000. So the potential capital gain would be $450,000: half of the original cost, $300,000, divided by two equals $150,000, stepped-up on the deceased spouse's half ownership of $600,000, for a total cost basis of $750,000.

The surviving spouse could use the IRS section 121 exclusion on the sale of a primary residence that has been owned and lived in for two out of the last five years to deduct $250,000 of the capital gain. (Remember, the spouse is now single, not married.) So the surviving spouse would be able to take the deduction to lower the capital gain amount by $250,000, down to $200,000 of taxable capital gain.

Let's assume a federal long-term capital gains tax rate of 20% and then another 3% for the state, for a combined capital gains tax rate on the sale of the home after the first spouse dies of 23%. The tax that would have to be paid would be $46,000.

Here's the math.

Sales Price of the Home	$1,200,000
Purchase Price	$250,000
Improvements	$50,000
Cost Basis	$300,000

One-Half Step-Up in Basis on Deceased Spouse

Sales Price $1.2M—One Half	$600,000
Surviving Spouse's Share of Cost Basis	$150,000
Surviving Spouse's Cost Basis ($600K+$150K)	$750,000
Capital Gain	$450,000
Section 121 Exclusion Available	$250,000
Taxable Gain	$200,000
Long-Term Capital Gains Rate (20%)	$40,000
State Capital Gains Rate (3%)	$6,000
Total Tax Surviving Spouse Will Owe	$46,000

Now, consider if the home had been re-titled back into the living trust after the refinance, where the bank required that it be taken out of the living trust and titled in the client's individual or joint names. The revocable living trust treats the ownership of the property as community property with rights of survivorship.

With the trust as the owner of the home, the tax benefits of the community property can be used. When one of the spouses passes away, the surviving spouse will be able to receive a full step-up in basis. A full step-up means that the cost basis will be raised to the full FMV as of the date of death. In the case of our example, that would be $1,200,000.

So consider the result. The surviving spouse can sell the home for $1,200,000, and she will not have a single dollar of capital gain. Her sales price is $1,200,000. Her cost basis is $1,200,000.

Zero capital gain. Zero capital gains tax. A tax savings of $46,000 just for making sure that you hold the title to your home inside of your living trust.

That's a very costly mistake!

Guess what? This tax savings does not apply to just your home. It can apply to:

- Rental and investment real estate
- Second homes
- Taxable investment accounts (stocks, bonds, mutual funds, and ETFs)
- Businesses you own
- Digital assets
- Other appreciated assets

The second common mistake we see in this space is when clients have investment brokerage accounts that are held in joint tenancy. The surviving spouse is limited to a step-up in basis on only one half of the capital gains in these accounts.

If the account has been properly titled in the revocable living trust in a community property state, then the spouse can receive a full step-up in basis to the FMV as of the date of death. This full step-up in basis is a move to tax-free—no capital gains. No federal or state taxes, and since the capital gain is reduced to zero, it does not make the surviving spouse's Social Security benefits taxable either.

Holding title to your assets with the right titling is so very key to being able to enjoy the tax benefits of community property tax laws.

Community property laws allow us to leave tax-free assets to our spouses.

The step-up in basis laws also provide the same full step-up in basis to our children and other beneficiaries when the second spouse dies and leaves these appreciable "**taxable assets**" to our loved ones.

When I say "taxable assets," the step-up in basis tax laws do not apply to tax-deferred accounts. Tax-deferred accounts include investments in traditional IRA accounts, 401(k)s, 403(b)s, 457 plans, defined benefit and cash balance plans, pension plans, ESOPs, deferred compensation, and just about any other tax-deferred retirement plan. Tax-deferred nonqualified annuities also do not qualify for a step-up in basis at the death of one of the owners.

These types of accounts will almost always force the beneficiaries to recognize and pay tax on those types of accounts as ordinary income—and at their full marginal tax rate.

Notice that tax-deferred permanent life insurance is not included in that list above. That is to say, under normal circumstances it is not.

Should you cash in a permanent life insurance policy early and make a profit on the life insurance policy, then those proceeds would also be subject to ordinary income tax rates.

However, in the case of permanent cash-value life insurance, if you use it as planned, the loans you take out, the accelerated death benefits for long-term care, and the death benefits you leave to your loved ones are income tax–free.

The same goes for the balances you leave to your loved ones in a Roth IRA. They are always income tax–free.

Here are some specific steps I recommend you consider taking.

1. Convert all retirement accounts to a Roth IRA. Leave them tax-free to your family. (You may leave some in the IRA enough that the RMD is covered by the standard deduction.)

2. Move all your taxable money to permanent life insurance retirement plans where possible. You will enjoy tax-free retirement income and leave the death benefits to your loved ones income tax–free as well.

3. Make sure you take advantage of community property laws for highly appreciated assets. Title the assets correctly in your living trust, and they will pass tax-free to the surviving spouse at the first death and then pass tax-free to your children at the passing of the surviving spouse.

So What About Estate Taxes?

Holding and enjoying tax-free income during your retirement is our first goal. Leaving assets income- and estate-tax-free to your heirs is our second goal.

The IRS has announced that the lifetime estate tax exemption amount in the United States for 2024 will be $13,610.000 per person. As the tax laws sit right now, in January 2026, the lifetime exclusion amount is due to sunset back to $5 million per person. The old $5 million limit will be adjusted for inflation, so many professionals expect it to be set around $6 million per person in 2026.[82]

That is what will happen unless the government takes some other action, like extending the Tax Cuts and Jobs Act of 2017. If they do not do so, then, without taking any action, the federal government will provide us with a huge tax increase in 2026 based on the projected new lower exemption amount.

People who have large taxable estates now or in the projected future can provide tax-free death benefits using permanent life insurance to cover the estate taxes that will come due at that time. Permanent cash-value life insurance is generally seen as the preferred vehicle to provide liquidity to pay the death taxes instead of having to sell an illiquid asset like the family farm, the family business, real estate, or private equity.

Providing tax-free methods to deal with estate taxes is beyond the scope of this book, but let me say that there is a complex array of charitable planning and other techniques to deal with estate tax liabilities. If you fear you will have a taxable estate, please make sure you are seeking the right professionals to deal with tax-planning opportunities, as there are many, and they can make all the difference between a huge tax liability and the family being left in a good situation.

---

82 Katherine L. Keating, "Increased Gift and Estate Tax Exemption Amounts for 2023," Foley & Lardner LLP, February 13, 2023, https://www.foley.com/en/insights/publications/2023/02/increased-gift-estate-tax-exemption-amounts-2023.

CHAPTER 17

MOMENTS OF TRUTH

Are You Prepared for Your Moments of Truth?

"By failing to prepare, you are preparing to fail."

—REV. H.K. WILLIAMS

We all experience moments of truth. A moment of truth may be the death of a loved one, an unexpected divorce, or the loss of a job. Other moments of truth may be a major change in our spouse's or life partner's health, or maybe a dramatic change in our own health.

Your dream team is meant to help you prepare for your own moments of truth—and to help you avoid costly tax and financial mistakes.

One mistake we often see involves a husband dying and leaving his 401(k) to his widow. His wife has several rollover options, including the ability to roll that 401(k) over into an IRA in her own name.

She can also name her own beneficiaries to that account.

Another moment of truth arrives when the second spouse passes away. Are the couple's children, the beneficiaries, ready, confident, and prepared to deal with settling the estate and the administration of their deceased parents' trust and estate?

Let's say that one of the children is a do-it-yourself investor—they want to set up the new accounts themselves and manage the administration of the trust themselves. They don't want any help. They know what's best, right? They are educated and smart. They don't want to use a financial advisor. They can do it themselves. They want to save money rather than using a professional tax or financial advisor.

The smart do-it-yourself son requests that the IRA company send him a check so he can roll over the IRA into his own account. The kid gets the check, puts it in his checking account, and then goes online to Schwab, or Vanguard, or whoever his online custodian is and opens a new traditional IRA account and deposits the funds into that new traditional IRA account.

However, the nightmare of such a moment of truth is that the new IRA should be an inherited IRA. The child has improperly set up that account. The son has made an excess contribution that must be withdrawn, and a 10% early distribution penalty must be paid. Additionally, what should have been an inherited IRA cannot be funded by a rollover like the son effected. What happened? This has gone horribly wrong.

As soon as the child took that distribution, the entire IRA balance became taxable. This is a very sad situation. All the parents' years of saving, scrimping, and waiting for the tax deferral to grow were destroyed in a single uninformed act, and now the full balance of the IRA is taxable all in one year, forcing the IRA to be taxed at the highest tax rate possible. The son, the beneficiary, lost all the future tax deferral.

When the son took possession of the distribution from the IRA, it was all over. He blew it up. There's no do-over or recovery from this mistake. And there's nothing he can do to make it better. He can't sue; he can't go to the IRS. It's checkmate. He's done, and he will most likely have to pay the very highest tax rate on the entire IRA balance, all in one year.

With proper advice, the beneficiaries could have set up an inherited IRA, and those funds could have been transferred via trustee-to-trustee transfer or direct transfer. That's what is required for the family to be able to maintain the tax-deferred benefits of the inherited IRA for beneficiaries.

You see, if you use the right tax and financial advisors, they can help you prepare your family for your own moment of truth.

Costly Mistakes

When I meet with clients to discuss estate planning and titling, we will typically have an estate planning attorney participate in the meeting, and the attorney will gather information about the client's wishes and then go back and draw up the legal documents for the client.

The living trust is just one of the documents that should be prepared as part of a client's whole legal package of documents. A will should also be included.

The biggest focus with estate planning is avoiding probate—keeping the courts from having to decide on your wishes. Attorney's probate fees could cost your relatives 4% to 7%, and with a $1 million estate, that comes out to $40,000 to $70,000.

Compare that to $3,000 to $5,000 to create a trust and all the other ancillary legal documents you need. One titling error could screw your loved ones out of a significant portion of your wealth when you die. Just like that.

Trusts and Pour-Over Wills

Another added benefit of a trust—which contains the couple's assets—is that it can pair with pour-over wills, meaning if you forgot to title something in the trust, such as a car, then upon your death, it will pour back over into the trust so your spouse can continue to use it.

All that planning will help you prepare for anything, even in cases where a financial power of attorney and medical power of attorney are needed. Wouldn't you prefer to have your wishes carried out instead of leaving those difficult decisions—such as whether to keep you alive in the hospital—to your spouse or children?

The Importance of Estate Planning

I think many of us don't want to discuss or think about our own mortality or any of the many bad things that could happen to us. One consideration that many parents of minor children don't know, or even consider, is that their wills determine who will be the guardian for their minor children, should the parents die prematurely.

Without a will, if, heaven forbid, a husband and wife were both to die in a car crash, their children could become the subject of a family fight. Who's going to raise the kids? His parents? Her parents? An aunt or uncle? We don't know with surety. It will be decided by the court after the couple is dead and gone, and their wishes may or may not be known or followed.

You don't want to leave all that stress and drama to your relatives.

Whatever your wishes, you need to put those wishes in writing. If you don't have a living will or advanced directive, then what you want does not matter because your wishes will never be known, much less followed. You will be forced to receive the default government plan. And take it from me: the default government plan is never the plan that you want or the plan that would be best for your family.

Ready for Anything

With couples, we will often see a division of labor. Maybe the husband takes care of the cars and pays the bills, while the wife cleans, cooks, and buys the groceries. The majority of the time, it seems like men tend to be more inclined to watch over the couple's investments—and they may steer the investments in a certain direction.

One spouse may be more focused on the investments and taxes, and the other may handle the family bills or other duties around the home. What happens if the financially focused spouse dies first? The other spouse leans on our expertise a lot more and values our insights. They have to step up and learn about the investments and be courageous and make important decisions.

It's not easy to gain—and cultivate—trust. As advisors who manage assets, we work as fiduciaries in the work we perform for clients. We have to walk our talk. We have to do what we say we're going to do. We have to be knowledgeable and competent in the advice we give so that our clients can experience firsthand the wisdom and experience we have to share.

That leap of faith to be able to trust your financial advisor is so valuable and important. It reminds me of the scene from *Indiana Jones and the Last Crusade* where Indy (Harrison Ford) is peering over the edge of a cliff, trying to figure out how to cross a deep pit.

"It's a leap of faith," he says, then sticks his foot out over the edge and steps onto an invisible bridge.

For clients seeking financial assistance, this process is akin to stepping out over the vast crevasse—you have to be willing to take your leap of faith, believing that the person helping you is telling you the truth and has your best interest at heart.

It's also similar, in a way, to a courtship, and seeing if you can spark the right match.

Is this the one?

Can I trust them with all my money?

Are they going to be true to me?

Are they going to honor me, and help me, and pick me up?

Are they going to have my best interest at heart?

Can they be trusted with my life's savings?

Or are they trying to sell me something and make money off me?

It's hard to overcome our natural skepticism. But it's vital to build trust in your professional advisors—because your trusted financial advisor just may be the most important advisor in your life.

There are sleazy advisors and attorneys out there. But I am applying for a different position with my wealth management clients. My team and I are applying to become our client's most trusted advisors. For taxes and tax planning, for investments and wealth management, for financial and retirement planning, and for legacy wishes and estate planning.

We want to be there so we can help clients and keep them from making costly mistakes.

Our track record helps in establishing trust, as do references and recommendations from other clients. But it really comes down to building a relationship and feeling comfortable about working together and establishing connections.

I hope you can build such a relationship with your team of advisors.

Being Prepared

Your "moment of truth" is foundational to everything we do for our clients.

I said it earlier, but it bears repeating: the Boy Scout motto, "Be Prepared," is foundational to my life's work.

As a financial planner, I don't want my clients to ever encounter unplanned surprises. I don't want them to ever be unprepared. That's not to say that surprises don't emerge—they are a part of life.

Our health will change at some point. I recognize that all too well—I've had my own health challenges just as everyone does sooner or later.

We have all faced our own surprises, moments of truth, if you will. And if you haven't yet, you will soon. It's a part of this life. When that someday arrives, and you have to face your own "moment of truth," the value of being prepared becomes apparent.

One of the biggest moments of truth arrives for each of us when we contemplate our own passing. If we have prepared properly for that moment, as difficult as it may be, our loved ones, including our surviving spouse, will be left with a level of peace, knowing that they are loved and have been provided for.

From Tears to Trust

Imagine a couple named Sandy and John. John had worked for an aerospace firm in the Northwest, and both Sandy and John had big 401(k) retirement plans. John had been all about investing in the stock markets, on the more aggressive side. Sandy, on the other hand, was more conservative about money—a lot more conservative—and was fearful of losing her life's savings, her nest egg.

Imagine when they first came in for one of their first appointments; there were tears. Tears of fear.

It's very emotional to take all your life savings and hand them over to somebody else.

Last year, John passed away unexpectedly—he had a heart attack in the hospital while waiting for heart surgery in the middle of COVID.

This year, Sandy decided that she wanted to secure a long-term care insurance policy for herself, so we've worked on purchasing an asset-based long-term care policy. One day, Sandy came back from a long trip and wanted to talk.

"I was having second thoughts," she told me. "Because if John was alive, he wouldn't have been in favor of this."

I said, "Sandy, this policy is here to protect you, and it is here to help make sure that you don't run through all your money on long-term care needs. An asset-based long-term care policy can help improve the chances that you can leave the legacy you desire to your children. That's what this policy does. And no matter what, this long-term care policy will be there when you need it for your own care, one way or another. If you die without needing long-term care, it may pay a tax-free death benefit to your children. If you need long-term care, it will be there for you. And if you change your mind and want to get most of your premium back, you may be able to do that too."

That's what makes my work so worthwhile.

We are helping people prepare for their own moments of truth—whether those moments come 20, 30, or even 40 years from now—because when the moment of truth arrives, the tax rates in the United States are most likely going to be much higher than they are today.

Your moment of truth may appear before you die, or it may show up at your death, when you leave your money to your spouse knowing that she will be well cared for. Or it may be the moment when the government has no choice but to raise your income taxes dramatically, like doubling them by as much as 50% or more.

That is very likely to happen.

Are you ready?

If you're already well on your way, then great!

If you're not, then let's get you ready.

CHAPTER 18

IN CLOSING

Your Move to Tax-Free Begins Today

"The time to repair the roof is when the sun is shining."
—JOHN F. KENNEDY

D o you have a crystal ball you use to predict the future? I sure don't.

But by moving to tax-free and being vigilant, you can plan for and diminish your future tax burden.

If you convert your IRA account to a Roth IRA, you have now taken the uncontrollable and you've controlled it. But if you don't do that, you're leaving yourself to face the government's mismanagement and all the consequences associated with that. They can come back and increase your taxes as much as they want, and there's nothing you can do about it.

If you have an IRA, or a 401(k), or a tax-deferred annuity that is not yet taxed, you are not going to be able to control how the government taxes those accounts in the future.

A Slice of Pie

I like to think of your life savings as a big pie. There's a slice that's going to come out of that pie for the federal and state government. If you structure this the right way, you can cut a pretty skinny piece for the government and keep the rest for yourself—but if you don't, over time, that skinny slice for the government is going to get wider and wider and wider.

And that's going to end up happening *no matter who's in office.* The government makes many promises, and many of them are empty. Politicians are going to have to choose between cutting benefits and raising taxes. And in the coming years, they're increasingly going to have to raise taxes.

People often think that the future tax rates will depend on whether Republicans or Democrats are in control of the White House and Congress.

But future politicians, regardless of party, aren't going to have a choice. Their hands are going to be tied, to a certain extent.

Whomever it will be at that point in the future, they will have to deal with:

1. The Medicare Hospital Insurance Trust Fund running out of money. (Projected for 2028.)

2. The Social Security trust fund running out of money. (Projected 2034 for OASI.)

3. The annual cost of paying the interest on the $34 trillion national debt at new higher interest rates. (6.8% of all federal

outlays in 2023.)[83]

4. Restocking our national defense supplies from the war in Ukraine.

5. All the profligate spending that our national government has had for decades.

6. World geopolitics that may require us (the United States) to participate in wars or conflicts that will require a lot of funds to support (e.g., potential conflicts in or with China/Taiwan, North Korea, Russia, Iran, or the Middle East).

No Surprises

Interest is consuming the entire U.S. budget, and the national debt is higher than it's ever been. The federal government is spending $1.5 trillion more than the revenue we have coming in every year. As that interest comes due on the national debt, it takes precedence over Social Security and Medicare, and it's bound to lead to increased taxes. Some politicians are going to resist that. But they're not going to have a choice; they will have to deal with the shortfall.

I don't want you to be surprised by that.

I hope that when this "moment of truth" occurs, your family is going to be protected from the rising taxes because you have moved to tax-free.

---

83 Drew DeSilver, "5 Facts about the U.S. National Debt," Pew Research Center, February 14, 2023, https://www.pewresearch.org/fact-tank/2023/02/14/facts-about-the-us-national-debt/.

Credit Crunch

This whole situation reminds me of a college student who gets approved for a credit card for the first time, and they use it like a debit card, charging things left and right. Then, when the bill comes due a few months later, they have no income to pay off the bill, and all of a sudden, they're buried in debt.

The problem for the United States is: we're the reserve currency of the world, and we have the petrodollar—which means that anybody who wants to buy oil in the world is paying for it in U.S. dollars.

State governments have to balance their budgets each year, and Americans have to balance their budgets in their households. The federal government, meanwhile, hasn't balanced its budget in decades. They just keep printing money. They keep spending on the national credit card and raising the debt limit.

But eventually, that bill is going to come due. And likely sooner than later.

My Wish for You

You will need help as you begin your move to tax-free, and I urge you to reach out to the right experts, whether you reach out to my team at www.Hoslerwm.com or me at www.movingtotaxfree.com or to local tax and financial professionals in your area. Start now so you can find and receive the higher level of advice you need and deserve.

You can connect with me at our website at www.movingtotaxfree.com.

No matter who you choose to work with, the most important thing is that you begin preparations today to start **moving to tax-free**.

Our government will not be able to keep all the promises they have made to you for social insurance benefits like Medicare and Social Security. When they have to choose between cutting benefits and raising taxes, I am hoping I have persuaded you to have as much of your investments already moved to tax-free vehicles as you can, so when that "*moment of truth*" arrives, you will be prepared, and your family will be protected from the harsh consequences of dramatically higher tax rates, inflation, and higher interest rates.

Wishing you every success as you begin your journey of moving to tax-free.

ACKNOWLEDGEMENTS

Over the last 27 years I have studied, learned, and worked long hard hours in the combined fields of tax, tax planning, financial planning, wealth and investment management, insurance, estate planning, and retirement planning. I would be remiss if I did not acknowledge the people and institutions that have been helpful in the creation of this work by their contributions to my learning and support in implementing the tools needed to help clients who are "Moving to Tax-Free."

I have been a member of the Ed Slott Master Elite IRA advisor group for 15-plus years. Ed is a master teacher and educator on all things concerning IRAs and retirement planning. I have attended this training twice a year in order to keep up on all of the tax law changes with IRAs and retirement plans. Ed's team has always provided accurate and timely information on the changes in IRA and retirement planning. Much of my expertise in retirement planning is due to the Ed Slott team and their ongoing education each year.

In 2024 I will begin my 20th year being affiliated with Commonwealth Financial Network. They are a class act as an organization. I can always count on Commonwealth to do the right thing. This book required tons of their time to get through the requirements of compliance, and yet the team at Commonwealth worked diligently with me to complete those requirements. My affiliation with Commonwealth has provided our firm with the ability to represent our clients in an objective and independent basis. I am honored to be affiliated with Commonwealth and their team of quality people.

I have been using the concepts of Moving to Tax-Free for more than 10 years. In that time, I have used and relied on the concepts taught by David McKnight in his book *The Power of Zero*. Even though I was never affiliated or worked with David McKnight until 2023, his thoughts, teachings, and writings are very closely aligned with my own. Many of my clients have such an amount and variety of income sources that they may never be able to get to the zero percent income tax bracket. Hence the name of my book is *Moving to Tax-Free*. I want to help people, even financially successful people, get as close to tax-free as they possibly can. Still, David's teachings, concepts, and general view of moving to tax-free have had a dramatic impact on my views and on the concepts I write about in this book. David is a great thought leader in this space, and I would be remiss if I did not acknowledge his contributions to this body of knowledge. It is my privilege to be affiliated with his organization The Power of Zero.

My team at Hosler Wealth Management certainly deserves credit for the fine work they perform, planning for and guiding our clients on their path of "Moving to Tax-Free." It takes a lot of hard work to track, prepare tax plans with options, and then implement the actions needed to help clients advance in their journey of moving to a tax-free retirement. Our team of hardworking, dedicated professionals provide our clients with a combination of high-level financial planning services that are not readily available anywhere else. I express my deepest gratitude to each and every one of our team members for their commitment to excellence and for their dedication to providing ever better, tax and financial planning results for our clients.

Disclosures:

This book was authored by financial advisor Bruce Hosler. He offers securities and advisory services through Commonwealth Financial Network®, Member FINRA/SIPC, a registered investment adviser. Fixed insurance products and services are separate from and not offered through Commonwealth Financial Network.

Tax and accounting services offered by Hosler Wealth Management, LLC, are separate from and unrelated to Commonwealth Financial Network.

Hosler Wealth Management, LLC, does not provide legal advice. You should consult a legal professional regarding your individual situation.

All investing involves risk, including the loss of principal. The investment strategies mentioned in this book may not be suitable for all investors, and there is no guarantee that your specific investment goals will be met. Asset allocation programs do not assure a profit or protect against loss in declining markets. No program can guarantee that any objective or goal will be achieved. Past performance is not indicative of future results.

LET'S KEEP THE CONVERSATION *GOING!*

Join the email list to receive exclusive content.
Visit **https://movingtotaxfree.com/**

For **special discounts** or bulk purchases,
contact **info@movingtotaxfree.com**

Book Bruce Hosler for
speaking events by contacting
info@movingtotaxfree.com

CONNECT WITH BRUCE HOSLER

Hosler Wealth Management

THANK YOU FOR READING!

If you enjoyed *Moving to Tax Free*, please leave a review on Goodreads or on the retailer site where you purchased this book and help me reach more readers like you.